Taste of Home
INSTANT POT®, AIR FRYER & SLOW COOKER
COOKBOOK

TASTE OF HOME BOOKS • RDA ENTHUSIAST BRANDS, LLC • MILWAUKEE, WI

Visit us at tasteofhome.com for other Taste of Home books and products.

ISBN: 978-1-62145-733-6

Executive Editor: Mark Hagen
Senior Art Director: Raeann Thompson
Editor: Amy Glander
Art Director: Holly Richmond
Senior Designer: Sophie Beck
Deputy Editor, Copy Desk: Dulcie Shoener
Copy Editor: Kara Dennison

COVER
Photographer: Mark Derse
Food Stylist: Josh Rink
Set Stylist: Stacey Genaw

Pictured on front cover:
Pulled Pork Sandwiches, p. 280

Pictured on back cover:
Maple-Dijon Salmon, p. 197
Lime Cheesecake, p. 100
Greek-Style Stuffed Peppers, p. 272

Printed in USA
1 3 5 7 9 10 8 6 4 2

ENCHILADAS, PAGE 295

LIFESAVERS FOR BUSY NIGHTS!

There's nothing quite like hot and hearty comfort food ready at the touch of a button. Now it's easier than ever to toss your favorite ingredients into one pot and watch dinner cook itself. Whether you own an electric pressure cooker, air fryer or slow cooker (or all three!), these are the appliances you can count on every day of the week.

With the **Taste of Home Instant Pot®, Air Fryer & Slow Cooker Cookbook,** you have over 150 delicious ways to harness the magic of these timesaving tools. Turn the page to savor popular party food, heartwarming Sunday dinner fare, potluck classics, speedy weeknight meals, superb sides, sweet treats and other family favorites that will have everyone coming back for more.

Thanks to their remarkable time and energy efficiency and ease of use, these versatile countertop cookers have become staples in the kitchens of cooks from coast to coast. Not sure how to get started? Tested, written and edited by the culinary pros at Taste of Home, this trusted source will guide you step-by-step on how to use these one-pot wonders with confidence.

Let **Instant Pot®, Air Fryer & Slow Cooker** take the stress out of serving up homemade goodness, even on your busiest nights. Dinner's done—let's eat!

CONTENTS

CHIPOTLE PORCUPINE MEATBALLS, PAGE 23

INSTANT POT®

Meet the kitchen appliance that's quickly become a best friend to today's busy home cook. From snacks and suppers to sides and sweets, electric pressure cookers make it a snap to serve hot hearty bites no matter how busy your schedule might be.

INSTANT POT® 101

Electric pressure cookers may seem intimidating at first. But with a little practice, patience and know-how, you can master this popular kitchen appliance like a pro.

- Read the instruction manual that came with your electric pressure cooker before you make anything. Not all brands and models are the same, so get to know your pot!

- For food safety and efficiency, never exceed the maximum level (also known as the max line or the fill line) indicated in the pot when adding food or liquid.

- Make sure the steam-release valve is closed before you start cooking. Even the pros at the *Taste of Home* Test Kitchen have forgotten to close the valve and returned to see the pot venting instead of building pressure.

- Check to be sure the steam-release valve feels loose to the touch. The steam-release handle works by applying pressure on the steam-release pipe. Because the contact between the handle and pipe is not fully sealed, the valve ma[illegible]se a little bit of steam whil[illegible]ood cooks.

- Pick up a pair [illegible]gs for safe, easy venting of your electric pressure cooker. Use the tongs to carefully turn the release valve—and keep your hands and face clear of the steam vent.

- The power cord on some models is removable, which makes the appliance easier to store. If you plug it in and the light doesn't go on, check to be sure the cord is attached securely. When the cooker isn't in use, consider storing the cord in the inner pot.

- After each use, remove and clean the sealing ring, steam-release valve and anti-block shield. See the opposite page for more cleaning tips.

- If your pot starts to smell like food even after cleaning it, put the sealing ring through the dishwasher. If that doesn't work, try steam-cleaning. Pour 2 cups water and 1 Tbsp. lemon zest into the inner pot. Place the lid on and run the steam program for 2 minutes. Carefully remove the sealing ring and let it air dry.

- Purchase extra sealing rings. Use one for your curries, tacos and other spicy dishes, and save the other for cheesecakes and other dishes with delicate flavors. Color-coded sets are available so you can always tell your savory and sweet sealing rings apart.

- The handles double as lid holders. Lid handles on newer models do double duty, holding the Instant Pot open with the lid out of the way. Not only is this great for the buffet line, it also lets you store the appliance uncovered to ensure the inside fully dries.

HERE'S HOW TO ADAPT YOUR OWN RECIPES:

PASTA. Cook for half the time called for on the package for boiling to al dente.

RICE. To substitute brown rice for white, increase liquid by ¼ cup and cook time by 5 minutes.

GRAVY. Increase the amount of cornstarch or flour a bit, since liquid won't evaporate in the cooker as it does with traditional cooking methods.

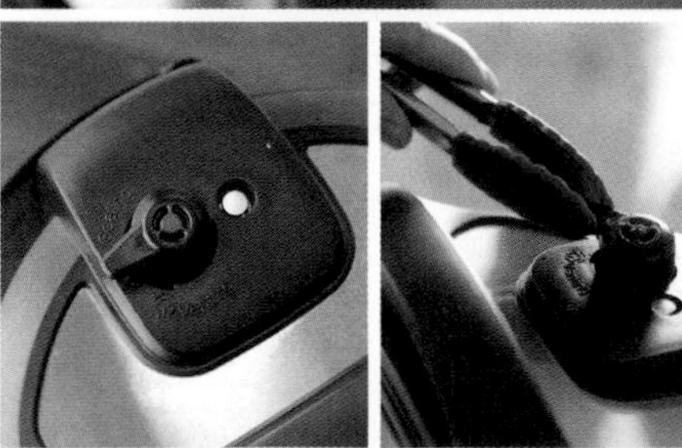

A. Appliance
B. Inner pot
C. Lid
D. Sealing ring
E. Anti-block shield
F. Condensation cup
G. Steam rack

CLEANING TIPS

- **Steam-Release Valve and Float Valve:** It's important to wipe food particles off these valves. You don't want anything to block the valves, because that would hinder the steam from releasing when you are cooking future meals.

- **Anti-Block Shield:** This is something that many cooks forget. Remove the shield from the lid. After hand-washing it, wipe it with a soft cloth and dry completely. Make sure to secure it in place on the lid before using the appliance.

- **Sealing Ring:** The sealing ring can absorb food odors, so you will want to clean it after every use. Wash by hand or in the dishwasher. Ensure it's completely dry before placing in the lid.

- **Exterior:** Wipe the exterior of your Instant Pot with a damp cloth as needed. It's important not to submerge the cooker in water since it contains the heating element. When you need to clean the inside of the cooker (not to be confused with the inner pot), use a damp cloth.

- **Lid:** After carefully removing the sealing ring and the anti-block shield, wash the lid on the top rack of your dishwasher. It is not necessary to clean the lid after every use, but it's not a bad idea to give it a good wipe with a clean towel between washes.

- **Condensation Cup:** This little cup collects the moisture that's created during the cooling process. It doesn't get particularly dirty, so a periodic wash is all it needs. You should check the cup regularly, however, and keep it clean with a quick wipe every now and again.

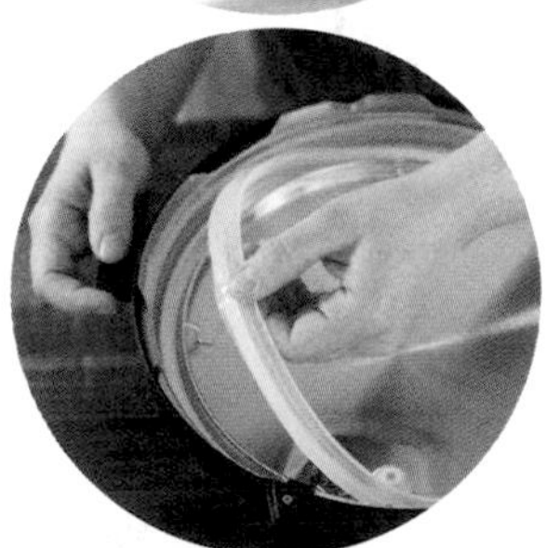

SNACKS

HEARTY PORK & BLACK
BEAN NACHOS, PAGE 15

BUFFALO CHICKEN DIP

BUFFALO CHICKEN DIP

If you like quick and easy recipes that are spicy, you'll love this chicken dip. It's super cheesy, easy and has that real Buffalo wing taste!
—Taste of Home *Test Kitchen*

PREP/COOK TIME: 20 MINUTES • MAKES: 6 CUPS

- 1 lb. boneless skinless chicken breasts
- 1 cup Buffalo wing sauce
- 2 Tbsp. unsalted butter
- 2 pkg. (8 oz. each) cream cheese, softened, cubed
- ½ cup ranch salad dressing
- ½ cup sour cream
- 2 cups shredded cheddar cheese, divided
- 5 Tbsp. crumbled blue cheese
- 1 green onion, sliced
- Tortilla chips

1. Place the first 3 ingredients in a 6-qt. electric pressure cooker. Lock lid; close pressure-release valve. Adjust to pressure-cook on high for 8 minutes. Quick-release pressure. A thermometer inserted in chicken should read at least 165°.

2. Remove chicken; shred with 2 forks. Return to pressure cooker. Stir in cream cheese, salad dressing, sour cream and 1 cup cheddar cheese. Sprinkle top with remaining cheddar cheese, blue cheese and green onions. Serve with tortilla chips.

¼ cup dip (calculated without chips): 173 cal., 15g fat (8g sat. fat), 44mg chol., 502mg sod., 2g carb. (1g sugars, 0 fiber), 8g pro.

HOISIN MEATBALLS

I love the start of fall because that means it's football season! Meatballs are filling and hearty and ideal for a tailgate. I served this for the first time at our favorite team's home opener. My best friend, who hates meatballs, couldn't get enough of them. I created a meatball convert! If you are serving children and prefer not to add the wine, use beef broth instead.

—Lisa de Perio, Dallas, TX

PREP: 20 MIN. • COOK: 10 MIN. • MAKES: ABOUT 2 DOZEN

- 1 cup dry red wine or beef broth
- 3 Tbsp. hoisin sauce
- 2 Tbsp. soy sauce
- 1 large egg, lightly beaten
- 4 green onions, chopped
- ¼ cup finely chopped onion
- ¼ cup minced fresh cilantro
- 2 garlic cloves, minced
- ½ tsp. salt
- ½ tsp. pepper
- 1 lb. ground beef
- 1 lb. ground pork
- Sesame seeds

1. In a 6-qt. electric pressure cooker, whisk together wine, hoisin sauce and soy sauce. Bring to a boil. Reduce heat; simmer until liquid is reduced slightly.

2. In a large bowl, combine next 7 ingredients. Add beef and pork; mix lightly but thoroughly. Shape into 1½-in. meatballs; place in cooker. Lock lid; make close pressure-release valve. Select manual setting; adjust pressure to high, and set time for 10 minutes.

3. When finished cooking, quick-release pressure. Sprinkle meatballs with sesame seeds.

Freeze option: Freeze cooled meatball mixture in freezer containers. To use, partially thaw in refrigerator overnight. Microwave, covered, on high until heated through, about 8 minutes, gently stirring halfway through.

1 meatball: 78 cal., 5g fat (2g sat. fat), 28mg chol., 156mg sod., 1g carb. (1g sugars, 0 fiber), 6g pro.

TEST KITCHEN TIP: The meatballs are a great appetizer, but you can enjoy them for dinner, too. Serve the hot meatballs over cooked pasta or rice for a quick savory entree. Add a green salad for a no-fuss menu.

HOISIN MEATBALLS

HEARTY PORK & BLACK BEAN NACHOS

HEARTY PORK & BLACK BEAN NACHOS

INSTANT POT®

My husband and I are both graduate students right now, so we don't have a lot of time to cook dinner. Our family loves this incredible nacho platter, and I love how easy it is to prepare.

—Faith Stokes, Chickamauga, GA

PREP: 15 MIN. • COOK: 40 MIN./BATCH + RELEASING • MAKES: 10 SERVINGS

- 1 pkg. (4 oz.) beef jerky
- 3 lbs. pork spareribs, cut into 2-rib sections
- 4 cans (15 oz. each) black beans, rinsed and drained
- 4 cups beef broth, divided
- 1 cup chopped onion
- 6 bacon strips, cooked and crumbled
- 4 tsp. minced garlic
- 1 tsp. crushed red pepper flakes
- Tortilla chips
- Optional toppings: Shredded cheddar cheese, sour cream, thinly sliced green onions, pickled jalapeno slices and chopped tomatoes

1. Pulse beef jerky in a food processor until finely ground. Working in batches, place 1½ pounds ribs in a 6-qt. electric pressure cooker; top with half the jerky, 2 cans beans, 2 cups broth, ½ cup onion, 3 bacon strips, 2 tsp. garlic and ½ tsp. red pepper flakes. Lock lid; close pressure-release valve. Adjust to pressure-cook on high for 40 minutes.

2. Allow pressure to naturally release for 10 minutes; quick-release any remaining pressure. Remove pork mixture from pressure cooker; make second batch by adding remaining ingredients to cooker. Repeat the previous procedure.

3. When cool enough to handle, remove meat from bones; discard bones. Shred meat with 2 forks; return to pressure cooker. Select saute setting and adjust for high heat; heat through. Strain pork mixture; discard juices. Serve with chips and toppings as desired.

1 serving: 469 cal., 24g fat (9g sat. fat), 87mg chol., 1055mg sod., 27g carb. (3g sugars, 7g fiber), 33g pro.

TEST KITCHEN TIP: Pinto and kidney beans work well in place of black beans. You can also try turkey jerky in place of beef jerky.

GARLIC-DILL DEVILED EGGS

Easter isn't complete without deviled eggs. I like to experiment with my recipes, and I was pleasantly surprised with how the fresh dill really perked up the flavor of these irresistible appetizers.

—Kami Horch, Calais, ME

PREP: 20 MIN. + CHILLING • COOK: 5 MIN. • MAKES: 2 DOZEN

- 1 cup cold water
- 12 large eggs
- 2/3 cup mayonnaise
- 4 tsp. dill pickle relish
- 2 tsp. snipped fresh dill
- 2 tsp. Dijon mustard
- 1 tsp. coarsely ground pepper
- 1/4 tsp. garlic powder
- 1/8 tsp. paprika or cayenne pepper
- Additional snipped fresh dill, optional

1. Pour water into 6-qt. electric pressure cooker. Place trivet in cooker; set eggs on trivet. Lock lid; close pressure-release valve. Pressure-cook on low for 5 minutes. Allow pressure to naturally release for 5 minutes; quick-release any remaining pressure. Immediately place eggs in a bowl of ice water to cool.

2. Cut eggs in half lengthwise. Remove yolks, reserving whites. In a bowl, mash yolks. Stir in all remaining ingredients except paprika. Spoon or pipe into egg whites.

3. Refrigerate, covered, at least 30 minutes before serving. Sprinkle with paprika and, if desired, additional dill.

1 stuffed egg half: 78 cal., 7g fat (1g sat. fat), 93mg chol., 86mg sod., 1g carb. (0 sugars, 0 fiber), 3g pro.

GARLIC-DILL
DEVILED EGGS

CLASSIC HUMMUS

CLASSIC HUMMUS

INSTANT POT®

We love hummus, and this version is amazing. If you have an electric pressure cooker, this is an easy, tasty reason to pull it out. We pair the hummus with fresh veggies for a quick snack.

—Monica and David Eichler, Lawrence, KS

PREP: 20 MIN. + SOAKING • COOK: 15 MIN. + CHILLING • MAKES: 2½ CUPS

- 1 cup dried garbanzo beans or chickpeas
- 1 medium onion, quartered
- 1 bay leaf
- 4 cups water
- ¼ cup minced fresh parsley
- ¼ cup lemon juice
- ¼ cup tahini
- 4 to 6 garlic cloves, minced
- 1 tsp. ground cumin
- ¾ tsp. salt
- ⅛ tsp. cayenne pepper
- ¼ cup olive oil
- Assorted fresh vegetables

1. Rinse and sort beans; soak according to package directions. Drain and rinse the beans, discarding liquid. Transfer to a 6-qt. electric pressure cooker; add onion, bay leaf and water.

2. Lock lid; close pressure-release valve. Adjust to pressure-cook on high for 12 minutes. Let pressure release naturally. Drain mixture, reserving ½ cup cooking liquid. Discard onion and bay leaf.

3. Place beans, parsley, lemon juice, tahini, garlic, cumin, salt and cayenne in a food processor; cover and process until smooth. While processing, gradually add oil in a steady stream. Add enough reserved cooking liquid to achieve desired consistency.

4. Cover and refrigerate for at least 1 hour. Serve with vegetables.

¼ cup: 139 cal., 10g fat (1g sat. fat), 0 chol., 190mg sod., 14g carb. (1g sugars, 6g fiber), 5g pro. **Diabetic exchanges:** 1½ fat, 1 starch.

CRANBERRY HOT WINGS

Cranberry wings remind me of all the wonderful celebrations and parties we've had through the years. My daughter's friends can't get enough of them.

—Noreen McCormick Danek, Cromwell, CT

PREP: 45 MIN. • COOK: 35 MIN. + BROILING • MAKES: ABOUT 4 DOZEN

- 1 can (14 oz.) jellied cranberry sauce
- ½ cup orange juice
- ¼ cup Louisiana-style hot sauce
- 2 Tbsp. soy sauce
- 2 Tbsp. honey
- 1 Tbsp. brown sugar
- 1 Tbsp. Dijon mustard
- 2 tsp. garlic powder
- 1 tsp. dried minced onion
- 1 garlic clove, minced
- 5 lbs. chicken wings (about 24 wings)
- 1 tsp. salt
- 4 tsp. cornstarch
- 2 Tbsp. cold water

1. Whisk together first 10 ingredients. For chicken, use a sharp knife to cut through 2 wing joints; discard wing tips. Place wing pieces in a 6-qt. electric pressure cooker; sprinkle with salt. Pour cranberry mixture over top. Lock lid; close pressure-release valve. Adjust pressure to high for 10 minutes. Quick-release pressure.

2. Remove wings to a 15x10x1-in. pan; arrange in a single layer. Preheat broiler. Meanwhile, skim fat from cooking juices in pressure cooker. Select saute setting and adjust for low heat. Bring juices to a boil; cook, stirring occasionally, until mixture is reduced by half, 20-25 minutes. In a small bowl, mix cornstarch and water until smooth; stir into juices. Return to a boil, stirring constantly; cook and stir until glaze is thickened, 1-2 minutes.

3. Broil wings 3-4 in. from heat until lightly browned, 2-3 minutes. Brush with glaze before serving. Serve with remaining glaze.

Note: Uncooked chicken wing sections (wingettes) may be substituted for whole chicken wings.

1 piece: 71 cal., 4g fat (1g sat. fat), 15mg chol., 122mg sod., 5g carb. (3g sugars, 0g fiber), 5g pro.

TEST KITCHEN TIP: You can substitute Sriracha for the hot sauce to switch things up a bit.

CRANBERRY HOT WINGS

CHIPOTLE PORCUPINE MEATBALLS

CHIPOTLE PORCUPINE MEATBALLS

My family loves porcupine meatballs. We have been eating this retro dish for years—I just updated it with a little more spice for myself. With the electric pressure cooker, it is ready in minutes and is perfect for a day when I don't have a lot of time. It makes some delicious leftover makeovers, too!

—Noelle Myers, Grand Forks, ND

PREP: 25 MIN. • COOK: 15 MIN. • MAKES: 1 DOZEN

- 1 large egg, lightly beaten
- ¾ cup uncooked instant rice
- 1 cup canned pumpkin, divided
- 1 envelope onion soup mix
- 3 Tbsp. minced chipotle peppers in adobo sauce, divided
- 1 tsp. Worcestershire sauce, divided
- 1 lb. ground beef
- 1 Tbsp. olive oil
- 1 garlic clove, minced
- 1 can (10½ oz.) condensed tomato soup, undiluted
- 1 cup beef stock
- ½ cup water
- 2 Tbsp. lime juice

1. In a large bowl combine egg, rice, ½ cup pumpkin, soup mix, 1½ Tbsp. chipotle pepper and ½ tsp. Worcestershire sauce. Add beef; mix lightly but thoroughly. Shape into twelve 2-in. balls.

2. Combine oil and garlic; place in a 6-qt. electric pressure cooker. Combine soup, stock, water, lime juice, remaining ½ cup pumpkin, 1½ Tbsp. chipotle pepper and ½ tsp. Worcestershire sauce. Pour 1½ cups sauce into pressure cooker; top with meatballs. Pour remaining sauce over top.

3. Lock lid; close pressure-release valve. Adjust to pressure cook on high for 15 minutes. Quick release pressure. Let stand 5 minutes before serving.

Freeze option: Freeze cooled meatball mixture in freezer containers. To use, partially thaw in refrigerator overnight. Heat through in a covered saucepan, stirring gently; add water if necessary.

1 meatball: 144 cal., 6g fat (2g sat. fat), 39mg chol., 397mg sod., 13g carb. (3g sugars, 1g fiber), 9g pro.

MARINATED MUSHROOMS

Here's a healthy addition to any buffet spread. Mushrooms and pearl onions seasoned with herbs, balsamic vinegar and red wine are fantastic on their own or alongside a tenderloin roast.
—Courtney Wilson, Fresno, CA

TAKES: 20 MIN. • MAKES: 5 CUPS

- 2 lbs. medium fresh mushrooms
- 1 pkg. (14.4 oz.) frozen pearl onions
- 4 garlic cloves, minced
- ¾ cup reduced-sodium beef broth
- ¼ cup dry red wine
- 3 Tbsp. balsamic vinegar
- 3 Tbsp. olive oil
- 1 tsp. salt
- 1 tsp. dried basil
- ½ tsp. dried thyme
- ½ tsp. pepper
- ¼ tsp. crushed red pepper flakes

Place mushrooms, onions and garlic in a 6-qt. electric pressure cooker. In a small bowl, whisk remaining ingredients; pour over mushrooms. Lock lid; close pressure-release valve. Adjust to pressure-cook on high for 4 minutes. Quick-release pressure.

1 serving: 43 cal., 2g fat (0 sat. fat), 0 chol., 138mg sod., 4g carb. (2g sugars, 0 fiber), 1g pro.

PEACH SALSA

Fresh peaches and tomatoes make my salsa a winner over store versions. You may need to prepare this recipe in two separate batches if it exceeds the maximum fill line on a 6-qt. pressure cooker.
—Peggi Stahnke, Cleveland, OH

TAKES: 25 MIN. • MAKES: 11 CUPS

- 4 lbs. (about 12) medium tomatoes, chopped
- 1 medium onion, chopped
- 4 jalapeno peppers, seeded and finely chopped
- ½ to ⅔ cup packed brown sugar
- ¼ cup minced fresh cilantro
- 4 garlic cloves, minced
- 1 tsp. salt
- 4 each chopped peeled fresh peaches (about 4 medium), divided
- 1 can (6 oz.) tomato paste

1. In a 6-qt. electric pressure cooker, combine the first 7 ingredients; stir in 2 cups peaches. Lock lid; make sure vent is closed. Select manual setting; adjust pressure to high, and set time for 3 minutes. When finished cooking, quick-release pressure according to manufacturer's directions.

2. Stir tomato paste and remaining peaches into pressure cooker. Cool. Transfer to covered containers. (If freezing, use freezer-safe containers and fill to within ½ in. of tops.) Refrigerate up to 1 week or freeze up to 12 months. Thaw frozen salsa in refrigerator before serving.

¼ cup: 28 cal., 0 fat (0 sat. fat), 0 chol., 59mg sod., 7g carb. (5g sugars, 0 fiber), 1g pro.

MARINATED MUSHROOMS

PORK PICADILLO
LETTUCE WRAPS

PORK PICADILLO LETTUCE WRAPS

Warm pork and cool, crisp lettuce are a combination born in culinary heaven. My spin on a lettuce wrap is loaded with scrumptious flavor and spice.

—Janice Elder, Charlotte, NC

PREP: 30 MIN. • COOK: 25 MIN. + RELEASING • MAKES: 2 DOZEN

- 3 garlic cloves, minced
- 1 Tbsp. chili powder
- 1 tsp. salt
- ½ tsp. pumpkin pie spice
- ½ tsp. ground cumin
- ½ tsp. pepper
- 2 pork tenderloins (1 lb. each)
- 1 large onion, chopped
- 1 small Granny Smith apple, peeled and chopped
- 1 small sweet red pepper, chopped
- 1 can (10 oz.) diced tomatoes and green chilies, undrained
- 1 cup water
- ½ cup golden raisins
- ½ cup chopped pimiento-stuffed olives
- 24 Bibb or Boston lettuce leaves
- ¼ cup slivered almonds, toasted

1. Mix garlic and seasonings; rub over pork. Transfer to a 6-qt. electric pressure cooker. Add onion, apple, sweet pepper, tomatoes and water. Lock lid; close pressure-release valve. Select manual setting; pressure-cook on high for 25 minutes. When finished cooking, allow pressure to naturally release for 10 minutes; quick-release any remaining pressure.

2. Remove pork; cool slightly. Shred meat into bite-size pieces; return to the pressure cooker.

3. Select saute setting and adjust for low heat. Stir in raisins and olives; heat through. Serve in lettuce leaves; sprinkle with almonds.

1 serving: 75 cal., 3g fat (1g sat. fat), 21mg chol., 232mg sod., 5g carb. (3g sugars, 1g fiber), 8g pro.

WHY YOU'LL LOVE IT...

"This is so awesome! So full of flavor. If you have picky children who don't eat a lot of veggies use tortillas instead of lettuce. They will love it! This is one of those recipes that will be a keeper and be made often."

—LMRAU, TASTEOFHOME.COM

SIDES

HOMEMADE CHICKEN & RICE SOUP, PAGE 39

SPICY COWBOY BEANS

SPICY COWBOY BEANS

These beans are a perfect contribution to a potluck buffet any time of year. Instead of hours on the stove, they cook quickly in the pressure cooker and there's no need to pre-soak the beans.

—Joan Hallford, North Richland Hills, TX

PREP: 25 MIN. • COOK: 1½ HOURS + RELEASING • MAKES: 10 SERVINGS

- 4 bacon strips, chopped
- 1 medium onion, chopped
- 2 garlic cloves, minced
- 2 cups reduced-sodium beef broth
- 3 cups water
- 1 pkg. (16 oz.) 16-bean soup mix
- 1 can (10 oz.) diced tomatoes and green chiles, undrained
- 1 can (8 oz.) tomato sauce
- 1 poblano pepper, chopped
- ¼ cup packed brown sugar
- 1 envelope taco seasoning
- TOPPINGS: Chopped fresh cilantro, shredded cheddar cheese and sour cream

1. Select saute or browning setting on a 6-qt. electric pressure cooker; adjust for medium heat. Cook bacon until crisp, 4-5 minutes. Add onion and garlic; cook until tender, 5-6 minutes longer. Add broth to pressure cooker. Cook 30 seconds, stirring to loosen browned bits from pan. Press cancel.

2. Add water, soup mix, tomatoes and green chiles, tomato sauce, poblano pepper, brown sugar and taco seasoning. Lock lid; close pressure-release valve. Adjust to pressure-cook on high for 90 minutes. Let the pressure release naturally.

3. If desired, select saute setting and adjust for low heat. Simmer, stirring constantly, until desired consistency. Press cancel. Serve with toppings of your choice.

Freeze option: Freeze cooled bean mixture in freezer containers. To use, partially thaw in refrigerator overnight. Heat through in a saucepan, stirring occasionally; add broth if necessary.

¾ cup: 245 cal., 6g fat (2g sat. fat), 10mg chol., 1823mg sod., 52g carb. (9g sugars, 21g fiber), 15g pro.

FRENCH ONION SOUP

I love French onion soup on a cold night, but I don't love the time it takes. This is my shortcut version for when we're low on time.

—Teri Rasey, Cadillac, MI

PREP: 20 MIN. • COOK: 15 MIN. • MAKES: 16 SERVINGS (4 QT.)

- ⅓ cup butter
- 3 lbs. onions, thinly sliced (10 cups)
- 2 garlic cloves, minced
- 2 Tbsp. sugar
- 4 cups beef stock
- 4 cups chicken stock
- ¾ cup white wine
- 1 tsp. salt
- Optional: Salad croutons and grated Parmesan cheese

1. Select saute setting on a 6-qt. electric pressure cooker and adjust for medium heat; add butter. Add onion; cook and stir until tender, 6-8 minutes. Add garlic and sugar; cook 6 minutes longer. Stir in stocks, wine and salt. Press cancel. Lock lid; close pressure-release valve. Adjust to pressure-cook on high for 8 minutes.

2. Let pressure release naturally for 3 minutes; quick-release any remaining pressure. If desired, serve with croutons and Parmesan cheese.

1 cup: 87 cal., 4g fat (2g sat. fat), 10mg chol., 724mg sod., 9g carb. (6g sugars, 1g fiber), 2g pro.

LEMON RED POTATOES

Butter, lemon juice, parsley and chives enhance this simple side dish. I usually prepare these potatoes when I'm having company. Since they cook in the pressure cooker, there's plenty of room on the stove for other dishes.

—Tara Branham, Austin, TX

TAKES: 25 MIN. • MAKES: 6 SERVINGS

- 1½ lbs. medium red potatoes
- ¼ cup butter, melted
- 3 Tbsp. minced fresh parsley
- 1 Tbsp. lemon juice
- 1 Tbsp. minced chives
- Salt and pepper to taste

1. Cut a strip of peel around the middle of each potato. Place potatoes and ¼ cup water in a 6-qt. electric pressure cooker. Lock lid; close pressure-release valve. Adjust to pressure-cook on high, 12 minutes. Quick-release pressure. Drain any cooking liquid; transfer potatoes to large bowl.

2. In a small bowl, combine butter, parsley, lemon juice and chives. Pour over potatoes; toss to coat. Sprinkle with salt and pepper.

1 serving: 150 cal., 8g fat (5g sat. fat), 20mg chol., 85mg sod., 18g carb. (1g sugars, 2g fiber), 2g pro.

FRENCH ONION SOUP

CHEESY BACON SPAGHETTI SQUASH

CHEESY BACON SPAGHETTI SQUASH

This quick side dish is called cheesy for a reason! Stir in any kind of cheese you have in the fridge.
—Jean Williams, Stillwater, OK

TAKES: 30 MIN. • MAKES: 4 SERVINGS

- 1 large spaghetti squash (3½ lbs.)
- 4 bacon strips, chopped
- 3 Tbsp. butter
- 1 Tbsp. brown sugar
- ½ tsp. salt
- ¼ tsp. pepper
- ½ cup shredded Swiss cheese

1. Halve squash lengthwise; remove and discard seeds. Place trivet insert and 1 cup water in a 6-qt. electric pressure cooker. Place squash, cut side down, on trivet. Lock lid; close pressure-release valve. Adjust to pressure-cook on high for 7 minutes. Quick-release pressure. Remove squash, trivet and water from cooker.

2. Select saute setting and adjust for medium heat; add bacon, stirring occasionally, and cook until crisp. With a slotted spoon, remove bacon to paper towels; reserve drippings. Stir in butter, brown sugar, salt and pepper. Separate squash strands with a fork and add to cooker; toss and heat through. Press cancel. Transfer to a serving bowl; stir in cheese. Top with the bacon.

1 cup: 383 cal., 26g fat (12g sat. fat), 54mg chol., 643mg sod., 31g carb. (4g sugars, 6g fiber), 10g pro.

WHY YOU'LL LOVE IT...

"Love the touch of brown sugar in the squash. Really good."

—WAGONDORFER, TASTEOFHOME.COM

EASY CORN CHOWDER

Enjoy this chowder's rich, slow-simmered flavor in record time by using a pressure cooker. Corn chowder is a classic staple, with its hearty flavors of creamy sweet corn, bacon crumbles, shredded cheddar cheese and chopped parsley.

—Taste of Home *Test Kitchen*

TAKES: 30 MIN. • MAKES: 8 SERVINGS (2 QT.)

- 4 medium red potatoes, peeled and cut into ½-in. cubes (about 2½ cups)
- 2 cans (14½ oz. each) chicken broth
- 3 cups fresh or frozen corn
- 1 medium onion, chopped
- 3 garlic cloves, minced
- ½ tsp. salt
- ½ tsp. pepper
- 2 Tbsp. cornstarch
- 1 cup half-and-half cream
- 1 cup shredded cheddar cheese
- 6 bacon strips, cooked and crumbled
- Chopped fresh parsley

1. Place first 7 ingredients in a 6-qt. electric pressure cooker. Lock lid; close pressure-release valve. Adjust to pressure-cook on high for 15 minutes. Quick-release pressure.

2. Select saute setting and adjust for low heat. Mix cornstarch and cream until smooth; stir into soup. Cook and stir until slightly thickened, 6-8 minutes. Stir in cheese and bacon. Heat through until cheese is melted. Press cancel. Sprinkle servings with parsley and, if desired, additional cheese and bacon.

1 cup: 191 cal., 9g fat (5g sat. fat), 31mg chol., 709mg sod., 21g carb. (5g sugars, 2g fiber), 7g pro.
Diabetic exchanges: 1½ starch, 1 medium-fat meat, ½ fat.

EASY CORN
CHOWDER

HOMEMADE CHICKEN & RICE SOUP

HOMEMADE CHICKEN & RICE SOUP

We love chicken and rice soup and thought it would make a superb pressure-cooker recipe. We were right!
—Taste of Home *Test Kitchen*

PREP: 10 MIN. • COOK: 5 MIN. • MAKES: 10 SERVINGS (2½ QT.)

- 3 qt. chicken broth or water
- 4 bone-in chicken breast halves (about 3 lbs.)
- ¾ tsp. salt
- ¼ tsp. pepper
- ¼ tsp. poultry seasoning
- 1 tsp. chicken bouillon granules
- 3 medium carrots, chopped
- 2 celery ribs, chopped
- 1 small onion, chopped
- ½ cup uncooked long grain rice
- Minced fresh parsley, optional

1. In a 6-qt. electric pressure cooker, place all ingredients. Lock lid; close pressure-release valve. Adjust to pressure-cook on low for 5 minutes; quick-release pressure.

2. With a slotted spoon, remove chicken. When cool enough to handle, remove meat from bones; discard skin and bones. Cut chicken into bite-sized pieces. Skim fat from broth; add chicken. Select saute setting and adjust for high heat; cook until chicken is heated through. If desired, sprinkle with parsley.

1 cup: 223 cal., 7g fat (2g sat. fat), 72mg chol., 1690mg sod., 12g carb. (3g sugars, 1g fiber), 26g pro.

CELEBRATION BRUSSELS SPROUTS

This recipe hits all the flavor points and makes a fantastic side throughout the year. Plus, you've got to love a dish that requires minimal effort and doesn't take up oven space. You can always omit the bacon if you need a vegetarian option.

—Lauren McAnelly, Des Moines, IA

PREP: 20 MIN. • COOK: 5 MIN. + RELEASING • MAKES: 10 SERVINGS

- 2 lbs. fresh Brussels sprouts, sliced
- 2 large apples (Fuji or Braeburn), chopped
- ⅓ cup dried cranberries
- 8 bacon strips, cooked and crumbled, divided
- ⅓ cup cider vinegar
- ¼ cup maple syrup
- 2 Tbsp. olive oil
- 1 tsp. salt
- ½ tsp. coarsely ground pepper
- ¾ cup chopped hazelnuts or pecans, toasted

Combine Brussels sprouts, apples, cranberries and half the crumbled bacon. In a small bowl, whisk vinegar, syrup, oil, salt and pepper; pour over Brussels sprouts mixture, tossing to coat. Transfer to a 6-qt. electric pressure cooker. Lock lid; close pressure-release valve. Adjust to pressure-cook on high for 3 minutes. Quick-release pressure. To serve, sprinkle with hazelnuts and remaining bacon.

1 serving: 204 cal., 11g fat (2g sat. fat), 7mg chol., 375mg sod., 24g carb. (15g sugars, 5g fiber), 6g pro.

TEST KITCHEN TIP: To shave Brussels sprouts, trim off the ends and put them in your food processor or slice with a mandoline. Or trim, halve and slice using a very sharp knife.

CELEBRATION
BRUSSELS SPROUTS

CURRIED
PUMPKIN RISOTTO

CURRIED PUMPKIN RISOTTO

This easy pumpkin risotto tastes like fall and gets a flavor boost from the curry.
—Andrea Reaves, Stephens City, VA

PREP: 10 MIN. • COOK: 15 MIN. • MAKES: 6 SERVINGS

- 1 Tbsp. olive oil
- 1 small onion, chopped
- 1 cup uncooked arborio rice
- 2 garlic cloves, minced
- 2 cups chicken stock
- ½ cup canned pumpkin
- 1 Tbsp. curry powder
- 1½ tsp. minced fresh rosemary or ¾ tsp. dried rosemary, crushed
- ½ tsp. salt
- ¼ tsp. pepper

1. Select saute setting on a 6-qt. electric pressure cooker. Adjust for medium heat; add oil. When the oil is hot, cook and stir the onion until crisp-tender, 5-7 minutes. Add rice and garlic; cook and stir until rice is coated, roughly 1-2 minutes. Add stock; cook 1 minute, stirring to loosen browned bits from pan. Press cancel.

2. Stir in pumpkin, curry powder, rosemary, salt and pepper. Lock lid; close pressure-release valve. Adjust to pressure-cook on high for 7 minutes. Quick-release pressure. If desired, serve with additional minced rosemary.

½ cup: 163 cal., 3g fat (0 sat. fat), 0 chol., 369mg sod., 30g carb. (2g sugars, 2g fiber), 4g pro.
Diabetic exchanges: 2 starch, ½ fat.

TRULY TASTY TURNIP GREENS

These savory greens are a hit at every church dinner. Adjust the seasonings as you please to make the recipe your own.
—Amy Inman, Hiddenite, NC

PREP: 20 MIN. • COOK: 5 MIN. + RELEASING • MAKES: 14 SERVINGS

- 2 lbs. peeled turnips, cut into ½-in. cubes
- 12 oz. fresh turnip greens
- 8 oz. fully cooked country ham or 2 smoked ham hocks
- 1 medium onion, chopped
- 3 Tbsp. sugar
- 1½ tsp. coarsely ground pepper
- ¾ tsp. salt
- 2 cartons (32 oz. each) chicken broth

1. In a 6-qt. electric pressure cooker, combine all ingredients. Lock lid; close pressure-release valve. Adjust to pressure-cook on high for 5 minutes. Allow pressure to naturally release for 10 minutes, then quick-release any remaining pressure.

2. If using ham hocks, remove meat from bones when cool enough to handle; cut ham into small pieces and return to pressure cooker. Serve side dish with a slotted spoon.

¾ cup: 63 cal., 1g fat (0 sat. fat), 11mg chol., 903mg sod., 9g carb. (6g sugars, 2g fiber), 5g pro.

ULTIMATE BLACK BEANS

Beans are the key to a lot of my family's meals, whether it's for a weekend breakfast or taco salads and burritos throughout the week. So I've been trying, for years, to find a homemade recipe as creamy and tasty as Mexican restaurant beans. This is that recipe.

—Helen Nelander, Boulder Creek, CA

PREP: 5 MIN. • COOK: 30 MIN. + RELEASING • MAKES: 20 SERVINGS

- 2 lbs. dried black beans (about 4½ cups)
- 4 tsp. salt, divided
- 12 cups water, divided
- ½ cup lard
- 1 Tbsp. ground cumin
- 2 tsp. garlic powder
- Optional: Queso fresco and cilantro

1. Rinse and sort beans. Transfer to a 6-qt. electric pressure cooker. Add 2 tsp. salt and 7 cups water. Lock lid; close pressure-release valve. Adjust to pressure-cook on high for 2 minutes. Allow pressure to naturally release for 20 minutes and then quick-release any remaining pressure.

2. Drain beans; discard liquid. Return beans to pressure cooker. Add remaining salt and water, lard, cumin and garlic powder. Lock lid; close pressure-release valve. Adjust to pressure-cook on high for 25 minutes. Allow pressure to naturally release for 10 minutes and then quick-release any remaining pressure; do not drain.

3. If desired, mash or puree beans in broth and sprinkle with queso fresco and cilantro.

½ cup: 203 cal., 6g fat (2g sat. fat), 5mg chol., 475mg sod., 29g carb. (1g sugars, 7g fiber), 10g pro.

TEST KITCHEN TIP: Lard makes for the tastiest beans, but vegetable shortening also works well. Just be sure not to omit the fat entirely, as it changes the texture of the beans.

ULTIMATE
BLACK BEANS

CHICKEN
TORTILLA SOUP

CHICKEN TORTILLA SOUP

Don't be shy about loading up the spices and shredded chicken into your pressure cooker. Chicken tortilla soup tastes great as leftovers the next day. Your family will thank you for this one!

—Karen Kelly, Germantown, MD

PREP: 10 MIN. • COOK: 30 MIN. • MAKES: 10 SERVINGS

- 1 Tbsp. canola oil
- 1 medium onion, chopped
- 3 garlic cloves, minced
- 1 lb. boneless skinless chicken breasts
- 1 carton (32 oz.) reduced-sodium chicken broth
- 1 can (15 oz.) black beans, rinsed and drained
- 1 can (14 oz.) fire-roasted diced tomatoes
- 1½ cups frozen corn
- 1 Tbsp. chili powder
- 1 Tbsp. ground cumin
- 1 tsp. paprika
- ½ tsp. salt
- ¼ tsp. pepper
- ¼ cup minced fresh cilantro
- Optional: Crumbled tortilla chips, chopped avocado, jalapeno peppers and lime wedges

1. Select saute setting on a 6-qt. electric pressure cooker and adjust for high heat; add oil. Add onion; cook and stir 6-8 minutes or until tender. Add garlic; cook 1 minute longer. Add the next 10 ingredients. Stir. Lock lid; close pressure-release valve.

2. Adjust to pressure-cook on high for 8 minutes. Allow pressure to naturally release for 12 minutes, then quick-release any remaining pressure.

3. Remove chicken from pressure cooker. Shred with 2 forks; return to pressure cooker. Stir in cilantro. If desired, serve with toppings.

1 cup: 141 cal., 3g fat (0 sat. fat), 25mg chol., 580mg sod., 15g carb. (3g sugars, 3g fiber), 14g pro.
Diabetic exchanges: 2 lean meat, 1 starch.

BBQ BAKED BEANS

I was under doctor's orders to reduce the amount sodium I was eating, but I just couldn't part with some of my favorite foods. After many experiments I came up with this potluck favorite—now everyone's happy!

—Sherrel Hendrix, Arkadelphia, AR

PREP: 10 MIN. + SOAKING • COOK: 35 MIN. + RELEASING • MAKES: 12 SERVINGS

- 1 pkg. (16 oz.) dried great northern beans
- 2 smoked ham hocks (about ½ lb. each)
- 2 cups water
- 1 medium onion, chopped
- 2 tsp. garlic powder, divided
- 2 tsp. onion powder, divided
- 1 cup barbecue sauce
- ¾ cup packed brown sugar
- ½ tsp. ground nutmeg
- ¼ tsp. ground cloves
- 2 tsp. hot pepper sauce, optional

1. Rinse and sort beans. Transfer to a 6-qt. electric pressure cooker. Add the ham hocks, water, onion, 1 tsp. garlic powder and 1 tsp. onion powder. Lock lid; close pressure-release valve. Adjust to pressure-cook on high for 30 minutes. Let pressure release naturally for 10 minutes; quick-release any remaining pressure.

2. Remove ham hocks; cool slightly. Cut meat into small cubes, discarding bones; return meat to pressure cooker. Stir in barbecue sauce, brown sugar, nutmeg, cloves, remaining garlic powder, remaining onion powder and, if desired, pepper sauce. Lock lid; close pressure-release valve. Adjust to pressure-cook on high for 3 minutes. Let pressure release naturally for 5 minutes; quick-release any remaining pressure.

½ cup: 238 cal., 1g fat (0 sat. fat), 4mg chol., 347mg sod., 48g carb. (22g sugars, 8g fiber), 10g pro.

TEST KITCHEN TIP: Using hot sauce to flavor foods can be a smart alternative to salt, but make sure you check the nutrition labels. We recommend Tabasco sauce. It has only 26 mg of sodium per 5-7 drops.

BBQ BAKED BEANS

ENTREES

HERBED CHICKEN & SHRIMP, PAGE 70

SPICED
SHORT RIBS

SPICED SHORT RIBS

This recipe is ideal for busy nights when your family wants a big dinner but you're limited on time. The ribs are tender and feature the perfect amount of sweet and sour. If you'd like, use red wine instead of chicken stock. And instead of butter, add more olive oil.
—Shanon Tranchina, Massapequa Park, NY

PREP: 20 MIN. • COOK: 40 MIN. + RELEASING • MAKES: 12 SERVINGS

- 1 Tbsp. olive oil
- 6 lbs. bone-in beef short ribs
- 2 Tbsp. butter
- 1 medium leek (white portion only), finely chopped
- 1 garlic clove, minced
- 1 cup chicken stock
- 1 can (6 oz.) tomato paste
- 2 Tbsp. ground mustard
- 2 Tbsp. red wine vinegar
- 2 Tbsp. Worcestershire sauce
- 2 tsp. paprika
- 2 tsp. celery salt
- 1 tsp. ground cinnamon
- ½ tsp. pepper

1. Select saute or browning setting on a 6-qt. electric pressure cooker. Adjust for medium heat; add oil. When oil is hot, brown ribs in batches; set aside.

2. Add butter to pressure cooker. When melted, add leek. Cook and stir leek until tender, 2-3 minutes. Add garlic; cook 1 minute longer. Add stock to pressure cooker. Cook 1 minute, stirring to loosen browned bits from pan. Press cancel.

3. In a small bowl, combine remaining ingredients; spread over ribs. Return ribs to pressure cooker. Lock lid; close pressure-release valve. Adjust to pressure-cook on high for 40 minutes. Let pressure release naturally.

1 serving: 232 cal., 14g fat (6g sat. fat), 60mg chol., 324mg sod., 5g carb. (2g sugars, 1g fiber), 20g pro.

COLA BBQ CHICKEN

My barbecue chicken is juicy and tender, and the sauce is filled with sweet, smoky deliciousness. Add a few tasty toppings to the sandwiches, such as sliced dill pickles and pepper jack cheese, for an additional boost of flavor.

—Ashley Lecker, Green Bay, WI

PREP: 10 MIN. • COOK: 10 MIN. • MAKES: 14 SERVINGS

- 1 bottle (18 oz.) barbecue sauce
- 1 cup cola
- 2 Tbsp. cider vinegar
- 1 tsp. garlic powder
- 1 tsp. onion powder
- 1 tsp. salt
- ½ tsp. pepper
- 2½ lbs. boneless skinless chicken breasts
- 14 hamburger buns, split
- 14 slices pepper jack cheese
- 1 cup sliced sweet pickles

1. Place the first 7 ingredients in a 6-qt. electric pressure cooker; add chicken. Lock lid; close pressure-release valve. Adjust to pressure-cook on high for 7 minutes. Quick-release pressure. A thermometer inserted in chicken should read at least 165°.

2. Remove chicken; cool slightly. Reserve 2 cups cooking juices; discard remaining juices. Shred chicken with 2 forks. Combine with reserved juices. Serve on buns with cheese and pickles.

Freeze option: Freeze cooled meat mixture in freezer containers. To use, partially thaw in refrigerator overnight. Heat through in a saucepan, stirring occasionally; add a little water if necessary.

1 sandwich: 367 cal., 10g fat (5g sat. fat), 66mg chol., 971mg sod., 41g carb. (18g sugars, 1g fiber), 26g pro.

COLA BBQ CHICKEN

ANDOUILLE RED BEANS & RICE

ANDOUILLE RED BEANS & RICE

When my husband's favorite New Orleans takeout restaurant closed, I challenged myself to develop a red beans and rice recipe I could make at home. This pressure-cooker version is tasty, hearty and satisfies his Cajun cravings. Serve it with sweet cornbread and honey butter.

—Jennifer Schwarzkopf, Oregon, WI

PREP: 20 MIN. • COOK: 40 MIN. + RELEASING • MAKES: 8 SERVINGS

6 cups water
1 lb. dried kidney beans
1 large onion, chopped
1 celery rib, sliced
½ medium sweet red pepper, chopped
½ medium green pepper, chopped
4 garlic cloves, minced
1 bay leaf
1 tsp. kosher salt
1 tsp. dried thyme
1 to 2 tsp. Louisiana-style hot sauce
½ tsp. pepper
1 lb. fully cooked andouille sausage links, sliced
Hot cooked rice
Thinly sliced green onions, optional

1. Place the first 12 ingredients in a 6-qt. electric pressure cooker. Lock lid; close pressure-release valve. Adjust to pressure-cook on high for 20 minutes. Quick-release pressure.

2. Stir in sausage. Lock lid; close pressure-release valve. Adjust to pressure-cook on high for 17 minutes. Let pressure release naturally. Remove bay leaf. Serve with rice and, if desired, sprinkle with green onions.

Freeze option: Freeze cooled bean mixture in freezer containers. To use, partially thaw in refrigerator overnight. Heat through in a saucepan, stirring occasionally; add water if necessary.

1¼ cups: 349 cal., 12g fat (4g sat. fat), 74mg chol., 774mg sod., 40g carb. (3g sugars, 9g fiber), 25g pro.

TEST KITCHEN TIP: This recipe tastes even better on the second and third day. If you can make it a day in advance, go for it—the sauce just gets thicker and tastier the longer it rests.

CORNBREAD STUFFED PORK CHOPS

Tart apple adds a delicious hint of autumn to the moist stuffing that fills these savory chops. The elegant entree looks fancy, but comes together in just an hour or less.
—Taste of Home *Test Kitchen*

PREP: 25 MIN. • COOK: 20 MIN. + RELEASING • MAKES: 2 SERVINGS

- 1 bacon strip, diced
- ¼ cup chopped onion
- ½ cup cornbread stuffing mix
- ½ cup chopped peeled tart apple
- 2 Tbsp. chopped pecans
- 2 Tbsp. raisins
- 2 Tbsp. plus 1 cup chicken broth, divided
- ¼ tsp. rubbed sage
- Dash ground allspice
- 2 bone-in pork loin chops (1 in. thick and 7 oz. each)
- 1 Tbsp. butter

1. Select saute setting on a 3- or 6-qt. electric pressure cooker. Adjust for medium heat; add bacon. Cook and stir until crisp. Remove with a slotted spoon; drain on paper towels. Add onion to drippings; cook and stir until tender, 3-4 minutes. Remove to a small bowl. Stir in stuffing mix, apple, pecans, raisins, 2 Tbsp. broth, sage, allspice and bacon. Cut a pocket in each pork chop by slicing almost to the bone. Fill with stuffing; secure with toothpicks.

2. Add butter to pressure cooker. When butter is hot, brown chops on both sides; remove and keep warm. Add remaining 1 cup broth to the pressure cooker. Cook 1 minute, stirring to loosen browned bits from pan. Press cancel.

3. Return pork chops to pan. Lock lid; close pressure-release valve. Adjust to pressure-cook on high for 18 minutes. Let pressure release naturally for 10 minutes; quick-release any remaining pressure. A thermometer inserted in pork should read at least 145°. Discard toothpicks before serving.

1 pork chop: 519 cal., 26g fat (9g sat. fat), 113mg chol., 1159mg sod., 21g carb. (12g sugars, 3g fiber), 37g pro.

CORNBREAD STUFFED
PORK CHOPS

SHREDDED CHICKEN TOSTADAS

SHREDDED CHICKEN TOSTADAS

These flavorful tostadas are super easy and family friendly. You won't believe how tender and juicy the chicken comes out. Just load up the tostadas with your favorite fresh toppings, and you'll have a simple, sensational meal.

—Lisa Kenny, Houston, TX

PREP: 10 MIN. • COOK: 3 HOURS • MAKES: 8 SERVINGS

- 2½ lbs. boneless skinless chicken breasts
- 1 envelope reduced-sodium taco seasoning
- 1 can (10 oz.) diced tomatoes and green chiles, undrained
- ½ tsp. salt
- 16 tostada shells
- 2 cups shredded Mexican cheese blend
- Optional: Shredded lettuce, chopped tomatoes, sliced avocado, sour cream, sliced jalapenos and fresh cilantro

1. Place ½ cup water in a 6-qt. electric pressure cooker. Add chicken and sprinkle with taco seasoning. Top with diced tomatoes and green chiles. Lock lid; close pressure-release valve. Adjust to pressure cook on high for 8 minutes. Let pressure release naturally for 10 minutes; quick-release any remaining pressure. A thermometer inserted into chicken should read at least 165°.

2. Shred meat with 2 forks. Return to pressure cooker and add salt; heat through. Serve on tostada shells with cheese and optional toppings as desired.

Freeze option: Freeze cooled meat mixture and juices in freezer containers. To use, partially thaw in refrigerator overnight. Heat through in a saucepan, stirring occasionally; add a little water if necessary.

2 tostadas: 378 cal., 17g fat (7g sat. fat), 103mg chol., 858mg sod., 18g carb. (1g sugars, 1g fiber), 36g pro.

SALMON WITH SPINACH SAUCE

You won't have to fish for compliments with this tasty recipe. The flavorful spinach sauce adds a pretty green accent to the pink salmon.
—Taste of Home *Test Kitchen*

TAKES: 20 MIN. • MAKES: 2 SERVINGS

- 5 oz. frozen chopped spinach, thawed and squeezed dry (about ½ cup)
- ⅓ cup mayonnaise
- 1½ tsp. Dijon mustard
- 1 tsp. lemon juice
- ⅛ tsp. garlic salt
- 2 salmon fillets (6 oz. each)
- ½ tsp. lemon-pepper seasoning
- 4 slices lemon

1. In a small bowl, combine spinach, mayonnaise, mustard, lemon juice and garlic salt; cover and refrigerate until serving.

2. Place trivet insert and 1 cup water in a 3- or 6-qt. electric pressure cooker. Place salmon on trivet; sprinkle with lemon pepper and top with lemon slices. Lock lid; close pressure-release valve. Adjust to pressure-cook on high for 3 minutes. Quick-release pressure. A thermometer inserted in fish should read at least 145°.

3. Discard lemon slices. Serve salmon with spinach sauce.

1 serving: 533 cal., 43g fat (7g sat. fat), 88mg chol., 617mg sod., 4g carb. (1g sugars, 2g fiber), 32g pro.

TEQUILA SALSA CHICKEN

I tried this dish at a local Mexican restaurant while celebrating a friend's birthday. I fell in love with the spicy, smoky flavor from the tequila and decided to try it at home in my pressure cooker.
—Trisha Kruse, Eagle, ID

TAKES: 15 MIN. • MAKES: 3 CUPS

- 1 envelope taco seasoning
- 1 lb. boneless skinless chicken breasts
- 1 cup chunky salsa
- ¼ cup tequila
- Hot cooked rice
- Optional: Avocado slices, chopped fresh cilantro and lime wedges

1. Sprinkle taco seasoning over chicken breasts; place in a 6-qt. electric pressure cooker. Combine salsa and tequila; pour over chicken. Lock lid; close pressure-release valve. Adjust to pressure-cook on high for 6 minutes. Quick-release pressure. A thermometer inserted in chicken should read at least 165°.

2. Remove chicken. When cool enough to handle, shred meat with 2 forks; return to pressure cooker. Serve with rice and desired toppings.

¾ cup: 187 cal., 3g fat (1g sat. fat), 63mg chol., 1107mg sod., 11g carb. (2g sugars, 0 fiber), 23g pro.

SALMON WITH
SPINACH SAUCE

PORK & CABBAGE DINNER

PORK & CABBAGE DINNER

This classic slow-cooker recipe was adapted for the new pressure cookers by the Test Kitchen. Either way, it makes an excellent option on busy weeknights. The meal is complete with vegetables but is also satisfying with a side of your family's favorite potatoes.

—Trina Hinkel, Minneapolis, MN

PREP: 15 MIN. • COOK: 55 MIN. + RELEASING • MAKES: 8 SERVINGS

- 1½ cups water
- 1 envelope onion soup mix
- 2 garlic cloves, minced
- ½ tsp. celery seed
- 1 boneless pork shoulder butt roast (4 to 5 lbs.)
- ½ tsp. salt
- ¼ tsp. pepper
- 1 small head cabbage (1½ lbs.), cut into 2-in. pieces
- 1 lb. medium carrots, halved lengthwise and cut into 2-in. pieces

1. Place water, soup mix, garlic and celery seed in a 6-qt. electric pressure cooker. Cut the roast in half; place in cooker. Sprinkle with salt and pepper. Lock lid; close pressure-release valve. Adjust to pressure-cook on high for 50 minutes. Let pressure release naturally for 10 minutes; quick-release any remaining pressure. A thermometer inserted in pork should read at least 145°.

2. Add cabbage and carrots to cooker. Lock lid; close pressure-release valve. Adjust pressure to pressure-cook on high for 5 minutes. Quick-release pressure.

3. Remove roast and vegetables to a serving plate; keep warm. If desired, skim fat and thicken cooking juices for gravy. Serve with roast.

1 serving: 424 cal., 23g fat (8g sat. fat), 135mg chol., 647mg sod., 13g carb. (6g sugars, 4g fiber), 40g pro.

TEST KITCHEN TIP: Pork shoulder is a flavorful cut with plenty of fatty marbling throughout. Trim any excess fat before cooking. The meat needs a longer cook time than most other pressure-cooker recipes to become tender.

MEMPHIS-STYLE RIBS

After my dad and I had dinner at the legendary Rendezvous restaurant in Memphis, I was inspired to create my own version of their famous dry-rub ribs. Smoked paprika in the rub mimics the flavor the ribs would get from grilling over hot coals.
—Matthew Hass, Ellison Bay, WI

PREP: 15 MIN. • COOK: 20 MIN+ RELEASING • MAKES: 6 SERVINGS

- ½ cup white vinegar
- ½ cup water
- 3 Tbsp. smoked paprika
- 2 Tbsp. brown sugar
- 2 tsp. salt
- 2 tsp. coarsely ground pepper
- 1 tsp. garlic powder
- 1 tsp. onion powder
- 1 tsp. ground cumin
- 1 tsp. ground mustard
- 1 tsp. dried thyme
- 1 tsp. dried oregano
- 1 tsp. celery salt
- ¾ tsp. cayenne pepper
- 2 racks pork baby back ribs (about 5 lbs.)

1. Combine vinegar and water; brush over ribs. Pour the remaining vinegar mixture into a 6-qt. electric pressure cooker. Mix together next 12 ingredients, reserving half. Sprinkle ribs with half of seasoning blend. Cut ribs into serving-size pieces; transfer to pressure cooker.

2. Lock lid; close pressure-release valve. Adjust to pressure-cook on high for 20 minutes. Allow pressure to naturally release for 10 minutes; quick-release any remaining pressure.

3. Remove ribs; skim fat from cooking juices. Using a clean brush, brush ribs generously with skimmed cooking juices; sprinkle with reserved seasoning. Serve ribs with remaining juices.

1 serving: 509 cal., 35g fat (13g sat. fat), 136mg chol., 1137mg sod., 8g carb. (5g sugars, 2g fiber), 38g pro.

MEMPHIS-STYLE RIBS

CAJUN CHICKEN ALFREDO

CAJUN CHICKEN ALFREDO

This is a true comfort food! Cajun spice adds a nice heat to the creamy Alfredo sauce. Add more or less seasoning depending on your preferred spice level. This pasta dish is also delicious with shrimp or smoked sausage.

—Jennifer Stowell, Deep River, IA

TAKES: 30 MIN. • MAKES: 6 SERVINGS

- 2 Tbsp. olive oil, divided
- 2 medium green peppers, chopped
- 2 boneless skinless chicken breasts (6 oz. each), cubed
- 2 Tbsp. Cajun seasoning, divided
- 1 pkg. (16 oz.) bow tie pasta
- 3 cups chicken stock
- 2 cups water
- 2 cups heavy whipping cream
- 1 cup shredded Parmesan cheese

1. Select saute setting on a 6-qt. electric pressure cooker and adjust for medium heat; add 1 Tbsp. oil. When oil is hot, cook and stir peppers until crisp-tender, 3-4 minutes. Remove and keep warm. Heat remaining 1 Tbsp. oil. Add chicken and 1 Tbsp. Cajun seasoning. Cook and stir until browned, 3-4 minutes. Press cancel.

2. Add pasta, stock and water (do not stir). Lock lid; close pressure-release valve. Adjust to pressure-cook on high for 6 minutes. Let pressure release naturally for 3 minutes; quick-release any remaining pressure.

3. Select saute setting and adjust for low heat. Stir in cream, Parmesan cheese, remaining 1 Tbsp. Cajun seasoning and cooked peppers. Cook until heated through (do not boil).

1⅔ cups: 717 cal., 40g fat (22g sat. fat), 131mg chol., 935mg sod., 60g carb. (6g sugars, 3g fiber), 31g pro.

HERBED CHICKEN & SHRIMP

Tender chicken and shrimp make a flavorful combination that's easy to prepare, yet elegant enough to serve at a dinner party. While I clean the house, it practically cooks itself. I serve it over hot cooked rice with crusty bread and a green salad.

—Diana Knight, Reno, NV

PREP: 15 MIN. • COOK: 30 MIN. + RELEASING • MAKES: 4 SERVINGS

- 1 tsp. salt
- 1 tsp. pepper
- 1 broiler/fryer chicken (3 to 4 lbs.), cut up and skin removed
- 1 Tbsp. canola oil
- 1 large onion, chopped
- 1 can (8 oz.) tomato sauce
- ½ cup white wine or chicken broth
- 1 garlic clove, minced
- 1 tsp. dried basil
- ¼ cup butter, softened
- 1 lb. uncooked shrimp (31-40 per lb.), peeled and deveined
- Hot cooked pasta, optional

1. Combine salt and pepper; rub over chicken pieces. Select saute setting on a 6-qt. electric pressure cooker. Adjust for medium heat. When oil is hot, working in batches, brown chicken on all sides.

2. In a bowl, combine next 5 ingredients; pour over the chicken pieces. Dot with butter. Lock lid and adjust to pressure-cook on high for 15 minutes. Let pressure release naturally for 10 minutes, then quick-release any remaining pressure. (A thermometer inserted in chicken should read at least 165°.)

3. Select saute setting; adjust for medium heat. Stir in shrimp. Cook until shrimp turn pink, about 5 minutes. Serve over pasta, if desired.

1 serving: 606 cal., 34g fat (13g sat. fat), 330mg chol., 1275mg sod., 7g carb. (3g sugars, 1g fiber), 61g pro.

HERBED CHICKEN
& SHRIMP

BEEF SHORT RIBS WITH CHUTNEY

BEEF SHORT RIBS WITH CHUTNEY

Tender, slow-roasted meat can be ready in half the time if you have the right equipment. I serve these savory beef short ribs over mashed potatoes, egg noodles or rice.
—Caitlin Marcellino, Apopka, FL

PREP: 30 MIN. • COOK: 35 MIN. + RELEASING • MAKES: 4 SERVINGS

- 1 tsp. olive oil
- 3 bacon strips, chopped
- 1 lb. boneless beef short ribs
- ½ tsp. salt
- ¼ tsp. pepper
- 1 lb. grape tomatoes
- 1 medium onion, chopped
- 3 garlic cloves, minced
- 2 cups water
- 1 cup Marsala wine or beef broth
- ¼ cup fig preserves
- 3 Tbsp. minced fresh rosemary or 1 Tbsp. dried rosemary, crushed

1. Select saute setting on a 6-qt. electric pressure cooker. Adjust for medium heat; add oil. When oil is hot, cook and stir bacon until crisp. Remove with a slotted spoon; drain on paper towels. Sprinkle ribs with salt and pepper. Brown on all sides in drippings. Remove from pressure cooker.

2. Add tomatoes, onion and garlic to drippings; cook and stir until crisp tender, 3-5 minutes, mashing tomatoes lightly. Stir in water, Marsala, preserves and rosemary. Cook 1 minute, stirring to loosen browned bits from the pan. Return ribs and bacon to pressure cooker. Press cancel. Lock lid; close pressure-release valve. Adjust to pressure-cook on high for 35 minutes. Let pressure release naturally. Remove ribs; shred with 2 forks and serve with reserved cooking juices.

1 serving: 368 cal., 19g fat (7g sat. fat), 60mg chol., 472mg sod., 25g carb. (18g sugars, 2g fiber), 19g pro.

WHY YOU'LL LOVE IT...

"This recipe reminded me of what my Mom made growing up. I used beef broth and next time I'm going to add some carrots and potatoes because this just reminds me of Mom's beef short rib stew. Don't be afraid to try this!"

—BUTCHER2BOY, TASTEOFHOME.COM

CHICKEN PAPRIKA

I appreciate the speed of the pressure cooker. I use it often to make these tender chicken breasts with a paprika-seasoned sauce that gets its richness from sour cream.

—Holly Ottum, Racine, WI

PREP: 15 MIN. • COOK: 15 MIN. + RELEASING • MAKES: 2 SERVINGS

- 2 bone-in chicken breast halves (about 2 lbs.)
- 1 small onion, chopped
- 1 cup chicken broth, divided
- 2 tsp. paprika
- 2 tsp. tomato paste
- 1 garlic clove, minced
- ¼ tsp. salt
- ¼ tsp. dried thyme
- Dash hot pepper sauce
- 1 Tbsp. all-purpose flour
- ½ cup sour cream

1. Place chicken in a 3- or 6-qt. electric pressure cooker; top with onion. In a small bowl, whisk ¾ cup broth, paprika, tomato paste, garlic, salt, thyme and hot pepper sauce; pour over chicken.

2. Lock lid; close pressure-release valve. Adjust to pressure-cook on high for 15 minutes. Let pressure release naturally for 10 minutes; quick-release any remaining pressure. A thermometer inserted into chicken should read at least 165°.

3. Remove chicken; keep warm. In a small bowl, whisk flour and remaining ¼ broth until smooth; stir into pressure cooker. Select saute setting and adjust for low heat. Simmer, stirring constantly, until thickened and sauce is slightly reduced, 8-10 minutes. Press cancel; stir in sour cream. Serve with chicken.

1 serving: 688 cal., 33g fat (13g sat. fat), 238mg chol., 999mg sod., 12g carb. (5g sugars, 2g fiber), 82g pro.

CHICKEN PAPRIKA

MEXICAN STUFFED PEPPERS

MEXICAN STUFFED PEPPERS

Traditional stuffed peppers get a southwestern twist! The filling also makes a delicious meat loaf that we enjoy cold as a sandwich with Mexican blend or cheddar cheese, mayo and salsa.

—Traci Wynne, Denver, PA

PREP: 20 MIN. • COOK: 15 MIN. + RELEASING • MAKES: 2 SERVINGS

- 2 medium sweet red, orange and/or yellow peppers
- 1 large egg, beaten
- ½ cup crushed tortilla chips
- ½ cup salsa
- ¼ cup finely chopped onion
- 2 Tbsp. minced fresh cilantro
- ½ tsp. ground cumin
- ½ tsp. seeded and finely chopped red chili pepper
- ¼ tsp. minced garlic
- ¼ lb. lean ground beef (90% lean)
- ¼ cup shredded Mexican cheese blend
- Sour cream

1. Place trivet insert and 1 cup water in a 3- or 6-qt. electric pressure cooker.

2. Cut and discard tops from peppers; remove seeds. In a small bowl, combine egg, chips, salsa, onion, cilantro, cumin, chili pepper and garlic. Crumble the beef over mixture and mix gently but thoroughly; spoon into peppers. Set the peppers on trivet.

3. Lock lid; close pressure-release valve. Adjust to pressure-cook on high for 12 minutes. Let pressure release naturally. Sprinkle peppers with cheese. Serve with sour cream and, if desired, additional salsa.

1 stuffed pepper: 319 cal., 15g fat (5g sat. fat), 141mg chol., 458mg sod., 25g carb. (8g sugars, 4g fiber), 20g pro.
Diabetic exchanges: 3 medium-fat meat, 1 starch, 1 vegetable.

SMOKED SALMON & DILL PENNE

I love making one-pot pastas in my pressure cooker. Every noodle soaks up the flavors of the delicious ingredients I toss in. I tried this version with some leftover smoked fish and fresh dill, and boom—this was born. It's now a staple in our house because it's on the table in half an hour and the kids love it!

—Shannon Dobos, Calgary, AB

TAKES: 20 MIN. • MAKES: 6 SERVINGS

- 2¼ cups chicken broth
- ½ lb. smoked salmon fillets, flaked
- ½ cup heavy whipping cream
- 2 Tbsp. snipped fresh dill
- ½ tsp. pepper
- 12 oz. uncooked penne pasta
- Optional: Additional dill and lemon slices

Place broth, salmon, cream, dill and pepper in a 6-qt. electric pressure cooker; top with penne (do not stir). Lock lid; close pressure-release valve. Adjust to pressure-cook on high for 8 minutes. Quick-release pressure. Gently stir before serving. If desired, top with additional dill and lemon slices.

1¼ cups: 322 cal., 10g fat (5g sat. fat), 33mg chol., 672mg sod., 42g carb. (3g sugars, 2g fiber), 15g pro.

CAROLINA-STYLE VINEGAR BBQ CHICKEN

I live in Georgia but I appreciate the tangy, sweet and slightly spicy taste of Carolina vinegar chicken.

—Ramona Parris, Canton, GA

TAKES: 25 MIN. • MAKES: 6 SERVINGS

- 2 cups water
- 1 cup white vinegar
- ¼ cup sugar
- 1 Tbsp. reduced-sodium chicken base
- 1 tsp. crushed red pepper flakes
- ¾ tsp. salt
- 1½ lbs. boneless skinless chicken breasts
- 6 whole wheat hamburger buns, split, optional

1. In a 6-qt. electric pressure cooker, mix the first 6 ingredients; add chicken. Lock lid and close the pressure-release valve. Adjust to pressure-cook on high for 5 minutes.

2. Allow pressure to naturally release for 8 minutes, then quick-release any remaining pressure.

3. Remove chicken and cool slightly. Reserve 1 cup cooking juices and discard remaining juices. Shred chicken with 2 forks. Combine with reserved juices. If desired, serve chicken mixture on buns.

½ cup: 135 cal., 3g fat (1g sat. fat), 63mg chol., 228mg sod., 3g carb. (3g sugars, 0 fiber), 23g pro.
Diabetic exchanges: 3 lean meat.

SMOKED SALMON & DILL PENNE

CHINESE-STYLE RIBS

CHINESE-STYLE RIBS

It's nice to come home after a long day's work and have dinner ready in a short amount of time. I hope you agree these ribs are quick, easy and delicious. Enjoy!
—Paula Marchesi, Lenhartsville, PA

PREP: 20 MIN. • COOK: 30 MIN. + RELEASING • MAKES: 6 SERVINGS

- 3 lbs. boneless country-style pork ribs
- 6 green onions, cut into 1-in. pieces
- 1 can (8 oz.) sliced water chestnuts, drained
- ¾ cup hoisin sauce
- ½ cup water
- 3 Tbsp. soy sauce
- 2 Tbsp. sherry or chicken stock
- 5 garlic cloves, minced
- 1 Tbsp. minced fresh gingerroot
- 1 Tbsp. light corn syrup
- 1 Tbsp. orange marmalade
- 1 tsp. pumpkin pie spice
- ½ tsp. crushed red pepper flakes
- 1 to 2 Tbsp. cornstarch
- 2 Tbsp. water
- Hot cooked rice, optional
- Thinly sliced green onions, optional

1. Place pork, green onions and water chestnuts in a 6-qt electric pressure cooker. Mix hoisin sauce, water, soy sauce, sherry, garlic, gingerroot, corn syrup, marmalade, pie spice and pepper flakes in a bowl. Pour over pork. Lock lid and close pressure-release valve. Adjust to pressure-cook on high for 25 minutes. Allow pressure to naturally release for 10 minutes and then quick-release any remaining pressure.

2. Remove pork to a serving platter; keep warm. Skim fat from cooking juices. Select saute setting and adjust for medium heat. Bring to a boil. In a small bowl, mix cornstarch and water until smooth. Gradually stir the cornstarch mixture into the pressure cooker. Bring to a boil; cook and stir until thickened, about 2 minutes.

3. Serve ribs with sauce and, if desired, rice and additional green onions.

1 serving: 493 cal., 22g fat (8g sat. fat), 132mg chol., 1115mg sod., 28g carb. (15g sugars, 2g fiber), 42g pro.

TEST KITCHEN TIP: Add ½ cup of water before cooking the pork to prevent high sugar ingredients from scorching on the bottom and meeting the minimum liquid requirements for this appliance.

PIZZA QUINOA CASSEROLE

Does your family look forward to pizza night? Switch it up with this quinoa casserole. It's a fun way to sneak in a healthy meal packed with protein and veggies.

—Julie Peterson, Crofton, MD

PREP: 15 MIN. • COOK: 10 MIN. • MAKES: 6 SERVINGS

- 1 Tbsp. olive oil
- ½ lb. Italian turkey sausage links, casings removed
- 1 small red onion, sliced
- 2 cups sliced fresh mushrooms
- 2 cups chicken broth
- 1 cup quinoa, rinsed
- 2 cups pizza sauce
- 1 pkg. (6 oz.) sliced turkey pepperoni
- 1 medium green pepper, chopped
- ½ cup shredded part-skim mozzarella cheese
- ½ cup shredded Parmesan cheese
- Optional: Minced fresh basil, sliced olives, oil-packed sun-dried tomatoes (drained), banana peppers and red pepper flakes

1. Select saute setting on a 6-qt. electric pressure cooker. Adjust for medium heat; add oil. When oil is hot, cook and stir sausage and onion until sausage is no longer pink and onion is tender, 5-7 minutes, breaking up sausage into crumbles; drain. Press cancel.

2. Stir in mushrooms and broth. Add quinoa (do not stir). Lock lid; close pressure-release valve. Adjust to pressure-cook on high for 2 minutes. Quick-release pressure.

3. Stir in pizza sauce, pepperoni and green pepper; cover and let stand until pepper softens slightly, 5-10 minutes. Sprinkle servings with cheeses. If desired, serve with optional toppings.

1¼ cups: 350 cal., 15g fat (5g sat. fat), 61mg chol., 1481mg sod., 30g carb. (6g sugars, 4g fiber), 25g pro.

TEST KITCHEN TIP: The natural coating on quinoa, called saponin, tastes bitter, so it's important to rinse it off. Most boxed quinoa comes already rinsed, but it won't hurt to give it an additional rinse.

PIZZA QUINOA CASSEROLE

PORK CHILI VERDE

PORK CHILI VERDE

Pork simmers with jalapenos, onion, green enchilada sauce and spices in this flavor-packed Mexican dish. It's fantastic on its own served over rice or stuff it in a warm tortilla with grated cheese, olives or sour cream on the side.

—Kimberly Burke, Chico, CA

PREP: 25 MIN. • COOK: 30 MIN+ RELEASING • MAKES: 8 SERVINGS

- 3 Tbsp. canola oil
- 1 boneless pork sirloin roast (3 lbs.), cut into 1-in. cubes
- 4 medium carrot, sliced
- 1 medium onion, thinly sliced
- 4 garlic cloves, minced
- 1 can (28 oz.) green enchilada sauce
- ¼ cup cold water
- 2 jalapeno pepper, seeded and chopped
- 1 cup minced fresh cilantro
- Hot cooked rice
- Flour tortillas (8 in.)

Select saute setting on a 6-qt. electric pressure cooker and adjust for high heat; add oil. In batches, saute pork, carrots, onion and garlic until browned. Press cancel. Return all items to the pressure cooker. Add enchilada sauce, water, jalapenos and cilantro. Lock lid; close pressure-release valve. Adjust to pressure-cook on high for 30 minutes. Allow pressure to naturally release for 10 minutes, then quick-release any remaining pressure. Serve with rice and tortillas.

Note: Wear disposable gloves when cutting hot peppers; the oils can burn skin. Avoid touching your face.

1 cup: 348 cal., 18g fat (4g sat. fat), 102mg chol., 580mg sod., 12g carb. (4g sugars, 1g fiber), 35g pro.

BEEF STEW

My family loves this pressure-cooker version of traditional beef stew. The roast and vegetables cook quickly and make a comforting meal. Try it with fresh rolls or crusty bread.

—Joanne Wright, Niles, MI

PREP: 15 MIN. • COOK: 50 MIN. + RELEASING • MAKES: 6 SERVINGS

- 1 boneless beef chuck roast (2 lbs.)
- 1 Tbsp. canola oil
- 5 cups water, divided
- 8 medium potatoes, peeled and quartered
- 4 medium carrots, halved widthwise
- 1 medium onion, quartered
- 1 tsp. minced garlic
- ¾ tsp. salt
- ½ tsp. pepper
- ½ tsp. dried thyme
- 2 bay leaves
- 2 to 3 Tbsp. cornstarch
- ¼ cup cold water

1. Select saute setting on a 6-qt. electric pressure cooker. Adjust for medium heat; add oil. When oil is hot, brown roast on all sides. Press cancel and remove roast. Place trivet insert and 4 cups water in pressure cooker. Set roast on trivet. Lock lid; close pressure-release valve. Adjust to pressure-cook on high for 40 minutes. Let pressure release naturally.

2. Remove roast and keep warm. Remove trivet. Skim fat from cooking juices and stir in remaining 1 cup water. Add potatoes, carrots, onion, garlic, salt, pepper, thyme, bay leaves. Lock lid; close pressure-release valve. Adjust to pressure-cook on high for 8 minutes. Quick-release pressure.

3. Remove vegetables with a slotted spoon; keep warm. Remove and discard bay leaves. In a small bowl, mix cornstarch and ¼ cup cold water until smooth; stir into pressure cooker. Select saute setting and adjust for low heat. Simmer, stirring constantly, until thickened, 1-2 minutes. Serve with roast and vegetables.

1 serving: 530 cal., 17g fat (6g sat. fat), 98mg chol., 403mg sod., 58g carb. (5g sugars, 8g fiber), 36g pro.

TEST KITCHEN TIP: This recipe can also be made in a stovetop pressure cooker following the same method.

BEEF STEW

EASY CORNED BEEF & CABBAGE

EASY CORNED BEEF & CABBAGE

I first tried this fuss-free way to cook traditional corned beef and cabbage for St. Patrick's Day a few years ago. Now it's a regular in my menu planning. Try it with Dijon mustard and crusty bread.

—Karen Waters, Laurel, MD

PREP: 15 MIN. • COOK: 70 MIN. + RELEASING • MAKES: 8 SERVINGS

- 1 medium onion, cut into wedges
- 4 large red potatoes
- 1 lb. fresh baby carrots
- 3 cups water
- 3 garlic cloves, minced
- 1 bay leaf
- 2 Tbsp. sugar
- 2 Tbsp. cider vinegar
- ½ tsp. pepper
- 1 corned beef brisket with spice packet (2½ to 3 lbs.), cut in half
- 1 small head cabbage, cut into wedges

1. Place onion, potatoes and carrots in a 6-qt. electric pressure cooker. Combine water, garlic, bay leaf, sugar, vinegar, pepper and contents of spice packet; pour over vegetables. Top with brisket and cabbage. Lock lid; close pressure-release valve. Adjust to pressure-cook on high for 70 minutes.

2. When finished cooking, allow pressure to naturally release for 10 minutes, then quick-release any remaining pressure. Discard bay leaf before serving.

1 serving: 414 cal., 19g fat (6g sat. fat), 97mg chol., 1191mg sod., 38g carb. (11g sugars, 6g fiber), 23g pro.

TEST KITCHEN TIP: This recipe may need to be prepared in two batches, as the corned beef brisket may exceed the maximum fill line on an electric pressure cooker when it's in one full piece. Simply cut the brisket into two equal pieces and cook separately.

SESAME CHICKEN

Your family will love the flavorful sauce that coats this chicken, and you'll love how quick and easy it is to make. If you serve gluten-free meals, use tamari instead of soy sauce.
—Karen Kelly, Germantown, MD

PREP/COOK TIME: 20 MIN. • MAKES: 4 SERVINGS

- 1½ lbs. boneless skinless chicken breasts, cut into 1-in. pieces
- 1 Tbsp. sesame oil
- ¼ cup honey
- ¼ cup soy sauce or gluten-free tamari soy sauce
- ¼ cup water
- 3 garlic cloves, minced
- ¼ tsp. crushed red pepper flakes
- 3 tsp. cornstarch
- 2 Tbsp. cold water
- 1 Tbsp. sesame seeds
- Hot cooked rice
- Thinly sliced green onions, optional

1. Select saute on a 6-qt. electric pressure cooker. Adjust for medium heat; add sesame oil. When oil is hot, brown chicken in batches. Press cancel. Return all to pressure cooker. In a small bowl, whisk honey, soy sauce, water, garlic and pepper flakes; stir into pressure cooker. Lock lid; close pressure-release valve. Adjust to pressure-cook on high for 4 minutes.

2. Quick-release pressure. In a small bowl, mix cornstarch and water until smooth; stir into pressure cooker. Select saute setting and adjust for low heat. Simmer, stirring constantly, until thickened, 1-2 minutes. Serve with rice. Sprinkle with sesame seeds and, if desired, green onions.

1 serving: 311 cal., 9g fat (2g sat. fat), 94mg chol., 1004mg sod., 20g carb. (17g sugars, 0 fiber), 37g pro.

WHY YOU'LL LOVE IT...

"My very picky teenage son loved this recipe. Mild but yummy flavor, good texture, and fast and easy because it's made in the Instant Pot."

—SHANNON HUDGENS SOEHL, TASTEOFHOME.COM

SESAME CHICKEN

DESSERTS

LIME CHEESECAKE, PAGE 100

BLACK & BLUE COBBLER

BLACK & BLUE COBBLER

It never occurred to me that I could bake a cobbler in my pressure cooker until I saw some recipes and decided to try my favorite fruity dessert recipe. It took a bit of experimenting, but the tasty results were well worth it.
—Martha Creveling, Orlando, FL

PREP: 15 MIN. • COOK: 15 MIN. + STANDING • MAKES: 6 SERVINGS

- 1 cup all-purpose flour
- 1½ cups sugar, divided
- 1 tsp. baking powder
- ¼ tsp. salt
- ¼ tsp. ground cinnamon
- ¼ tsp. ground nutmeg
- 2 large eggs, room temperature, lightly beaten
- 2 Tbsp. 2% milk
- 2 Tbsp. canola oil
- 2 cups fresh or frozen blackberries
- 2 cups fresh or frozen blueberries
- ¾ cup water
- 1 tsp. grated orange zest
- Optional: Whipped cream or vanilla ice cream

1. Place 1 cup of water in an 8-qt. electric pressure cooker.

2. In a large bowl, combine flour, ¾ cup sugar, baking powder, salt, cinnamon and nutmeg. Combine eggs, milk and oil; stir into dry ingredients just until moistened. Spread the batter evenly onto bottom of a greased 1½-qt. baking dish.

3. In a large saucepan, combine berries, water, orange zest and remaining sugar; bring to a boil. Remove from heat; immediately pour over batter. Place a piece of aluminum foil loosely on top of dish to prevent moisture from getting inside. Fold an 18x12-in. piece of foil lengthwise into thirds, making a sling. Place dish on a trivet; using foil sling, lower dish and trivet into pressure cooker. Lock lid; close pressure-release valve. Adjust to pressure-cook on high for 15 minutes. Allow pressure to naturally release for 10 minutes and then quick-release any remaining pressure.

4. Using sling, lift dish from pressure cooker. Uncover and let stand for 30 minutes before serving. Serve with whipped cream or ice cream if desired.

1 serving: 391 cal., 7g fat (1g sat. fat), 72mg chol., 190mg sod., 80g carb. (58g sugars, 4g fiber), 5g pro.

TEST KITCHEN TIP: This recipe was tested in an 8-qt. electric pressure cooker. For smaller cookers, recipes may need to be prepared in batches.

MIXED FRUIT & PISTACHIO CAKE

This cake is easy to make on a lazy day and a guaranteed-delicious dessert for several days, if you can make it last that long. It's wonderful for the fall and even the holidays.

—Nancy Heishman, Las Vegas, NV

PREP: 20 MIN. • COOK: 50 MIN. + RELEASING • MAKES: 8 SERVINGS

- 1½ cups all-purpose flour
- 1½ tsp. ground cinnamon
- ½ tsp. baking soda
- ½ tsp. baking powder
- ½ tsp. ground allspice
- ¼ tsp. salt
- 1 can (8 oz.) jellied cranberry sauce
- ⅓ cup packed brown sugar
- ⅓ cup buttermilk
- ¼ cup butter, melted
- 2 tsp. grated orange zest
- ½ tsp. orange extract
- 1 large egg, room temperature
- 1 cup mixed dried fruit bits
- 1 cup pistachios, chopped
- Optional: Whipped cream and additional chopped pistachios

1. Place 1 cup water into a 6-qt. electric pressure cooker.

2. In a bowl, whisk together dry ingredients. In another bowl, combine next 7 ingredients. Add cranberry mixture to flour mixture; stir until smooth. Add dried fruit and pistachios.

3. Pour batter into a greased 1½-qt. baking dish. Cover dish with aluminum foil. Place trivet insert in cooker. Fold an 18x12-in. piece of foil lengthwise into thirds, making a sling. Use sling to lower dish onto trivet. Lock lid; close pressure-release valve. Adjust to pressure-cook on high for 50 minutes.

4. Allow pressure to naturally release for 15 minutes, then quick-release any remaining pressure. A toothpick inserted in center should come out clean. Remove baking dish to a wire rack. Cool 30 minutes before inverting onto a serving platter.

5. Cut into wedges with a serrated knife; if desired, serve with whipped cream and additional pistachios.

1 serving: 385 cal., 14g fat (5g sat. fat), 39mg chol., 364mg sod., 59g carb. (32g sugars, 4g fiber), 7g pro.

MIXED FRUIT & PISTACHIO CAKE

MOLTEN MOCHA CAKE

MOLTEN MOCHA CAKE

When I first made my decadent chocolate cake, my husband's and daughter's expressions said it all. She says it's one of her favorites. Later, I took one of these to our next-door neighbors. Their teenage son, who answered the door, ate the whole thing without telling anyone else about it!
—Aimee Fortney, Fairview, TN

PREP: 10 MIN. • COOK: 25 MIN. + RELEASING • MAKES: 6 SERVINGS

- 1 cup water
- 4 large eggs, room temperature
- 1½ cups sugar
- ½ cup butter, melted
- 1 Tbsp. vanilla extract
- 1 cup all-purpose flour
- ½ cup baking cocoa
- 1 Tbsp. instant coffee granules
- ¼ tsp. salt
- Optional: Fresh raspberries or sliced fresh strawberries and vanilla ice cream

1. Pour water into a 6-qt. electric pressure cooker. In a large bowl, beat eggs, sugar, butter and vanilla until blended. In another bowl, whisk flour, cocoa, coffee granules and salt; gradually beat into egg mixture.

2. Transfer to a greased 1½-qt. baking dish. Cover loosely with foil to prevent moisture from getting into dish. Place on a trivet with handles; lower into the pressure cooker. Lock lid; close pressure-release valve. Adjust to pressure-cook on high for 25 minutes.

3. When finished cooking, allow pressure to naturally release for 10 minutes, then quick-release any remaining pressure. A toothpick should come out with moist crumbs. If desired, serve cake warm with berries and ice cream.

1 serving: 723 cal., 29g fat (16g sat. fat), 247mg chol., 403mg sod., 107g carb. (76g sugars, 3g fiber), 12g pro.

TEST KITCHEN TIP: Try topping this treat with caramel and chopped nuts for a turtle-flavored variation.

LIME CHEESECAKE

I love my pressure cooker and enjoy trying new recipes. I had been wanting to make a cheesecake, so I did a lot of research and finally came up with this recipe. It's a winner! The finished cheesecake was not only beautiful with no cracks, but also absolutely delicious.
—Joan Hallford, North Richland Hills, TX

PREP: 20 MIN. • COOK: 50 MIN. + COOLING • MAKES: 8 SERVINGS

- ¾ cup graham cracker crumbs
- 1 Tbsp. sugar
- 3 Tbsp. butter, melted

FILLING

- 2 pkg. (8 oz. each) cream cheese, softened
- ¾ cup sugar
- ¼ cup sour cream
- 2 to 3 tsp. grated lime zest
- 1 Tbsp. lime juice
- 1 tsp. vanilla extract
- 2 large eggs, room temperature, lightly beaten
- Optional: Lime slices and whipped cream

1. Place trivet insert and 1 cup water in a 6-qt. electric pressure cooker. Grease a 6-in. springform pan; place on a double thickness of heavy-duty foil (about 12 in. square). Wrap securely around pan.

2. In a small bowl, combine cracker crumbs and sugar. Stir in melted butter. Press onto bottom and up sides of prepared pan. Place in freezer. Meanwhile, in a large bowl, beat cream cheese and sugar until smooth. Beat in the sour cream, lime zest, lime juice and vanilla. Add eggs; beat on low speed just until blended. Pour into prepared pan. Cover pan with foil. Fold an 18x12-in. piece of foil lengthwise into thirds, making a sling. Use sling to lower pan onto trivet.

3. Lock lid; close pressure-release valve. Adjust to pressure-cook on high for 50 minutes. Let pressure release naturally for 10 minutes; quick-release any remaining pressure. Using foil sling, carefully remove springform pan. Let stand 10 minutes. Remove foil from pan. Cool cheesecake on a wire rack 1 hour.

4. Loosen sides from pan with a knife. Refrigerate overnight, covering when cooled. To serve, remove rim from springform pan. If desired, garnish with lime slices and whipped cream.

1 piece: 292 cal., 18g fat (10g sat. fat), 88mg chol., 187mg sod., 30g carb. (24g sugars, 0 fiber), 4g pro.

LIME
CHEESECAKE

APPLE COMFORT

APPLE COMFORT

When the temperature drops and winter rolls in, it's the perfect time for this warm and satisfying dessert.
—Awynne Thurstenson, Siloam Springs, AR

PREP: 30 MIN. • COOK: 12 MIN. + RELEASING • MAKES: 8 SERVINGS

- 1 cup water
- 6 medium tart apples, peeled and sliced
- 1 cup sugar
- ¼ cup all-purpose flour
- 2 tsp. ground cinnamon
- 2 large eggs
- 1 cup heavy whipping cream
- 1 tsp. vanilla extract
- 1 cup graham cracker crumbs
- ½ cup chopped pecans
- ¼ cup butter, melted
- Vanilla ice cream, optional

1. Add 1 cup water to a 6-qt. electric pressure cooker. In a large bowl, combine apples, sugar, flour and cinnamon. Spoon into a greased 1½-qt. souffle or round baking dish. In a small bowl, whisk eggs, cream and vanilla; pour over apple mixture. In another bowl, combine cracker crumbs, pecans and butter; sprinkle over top.

2. Loosely cover dish with foil to prevent moisture from getting into the dish. Place on a trivet with handles; lower into pressure cooker. Lock lid; close pressure-release valve. Adjust to pressure-cook on high for 12 minutes. When finished cooking, allow pressure to naturally release for 10 minutes, then quick-release any remaining pressure. Serve warm, with ice cream if desired.

1 serving: 433 cal., 24g fat (12g sat. fat), 96mg chol., 129mg sod., 53g carb. (40g sugars, 3g fiber), 5g pro.

TEST KITCHEN TIP: Choose an apple that will hold up to high temperatures. Granny Smith, Honeycrisp or Jonagold are fantastic options.

FLAN IN A JAR

Spoil yourself or the people you love with these delightful portable custards—a cute and fun take on the Mexican dessert classic. Tuck a jar into your lunchbox for a sweet treat.

—Megumi Garcia, Milwaukee, WI

PREP: 25 MIN. + COOLING • COOK: 10 MIN. + RELEASING • MAKES: 6 SERVINGS

- ½ cup sugar
- 1 Tbsp. hot water
- 1 cup coconut milk or whole milk
- ⅓ cup whole milk
- ⅓ cup sweetened condensed milk
- 2 large eggs plus 1 large egg yolk, lightly beaten
- Dash salt
- 1 tsp. vanilla extract
- 1 tsp. dark rum, optional

1. In a small heavy saucepan, spread sugar; cook, without stirring, over medium-low heat until it begins to melt. Gently drag melted sugar to center of pan so sugar melts evenly. Cook, stirring constantly, until melted sugar turns a deep amber color, about 2 minutes. Immediately remove from heat and carefully stir in hot water. Quickly pour into 6 hot 4-oz. jars.

2. In a small saucepan, heat coconut milk and whole milk until bubbles form around sides of pan; remove from heat. In a large bowl, whisk condensed milk, eggs, egg yolk and salt until blended but not foamy. Slowly stir in hot milk; stir in vanilla and, if desired, rum. Strain through a fine sieve. Pour egg mixture into prepared jars. Center lids on jars; screw on bands until fingertip tight.

3. Place trivet insert and 1 cup water in a 6-qt. electric pressure cooker. Place jars on trivet, offset-stacking as needed. Lock lid; close pressure-release valve. Adjust to pressure-cook on high for 6 minutes.

4. Let pressure release naturally for 10 minutes; quick-release any remaining pressure. Cool jars 30 minutes at room temperature. Refrigerate until cold, about 1 hour. Run a knife around sides of jars; gently invert flans onto dessert plates.

⅓ cup: 223 cal., 10g fat (8g sat. fat), 100mg chol., 306mg sod., 28g carb. (27g sugars, 0 fiber), 5g pro.

TEST KITCHEN TIP: You can use rum extract in place of the dark rum.

FLAN
IN A JAR

VERY VANILLA CHEESECAKE

VERY VANILLA CHEESECAKE

Cinnamon and vanilla give this cheesecake so much flavor, and making it in the pressure cooker creates a silky smooth texture that's hard to resist.
—*Krista Lanphier, Milwaukee, WI*

PREP: 20 MIN. • COOK: 65 MIN. + COOLING • MAKES: 6 SERVINGS

- 1 cup water
- ¾ cup graham cracker crumbs
- 1 Tbsp. plus ⅔ cup sugar, divided
- ¼ tsp. ground cinnamon
- 2½ Tbsp. butter, melted
- 2 pkg. (8 oz. each) cream cheese, softened
- 2 to 3 tsp. vanilla extract
- 2 large eggs, lightly beaten

TOPPING (OPTIONAL)

- 4 oz. white baking chocolate, chopped
- 3 Tbsp. heavy whipping cream
- Optional: Sliced kiwi and fresh berries

1. Grease a 6-in. springform pan; pour the water into a 6-qt. electric pressure cooker.

2. Mix cracker crumbs, 1 Tbsp. sugar and cinnamon; stir in butter. Press onto bottom and about 1 in. up sides of prepared pan.

3. In another bowl, beat cream cheese and remaining sugar until smooth. Beat in vanilla. Add eggs; beat on low speed just until combined. Pour over the crust.

4. Cover cheesecake tightly with foil. Place springform pan on a trivet with handles; lower into cooker. Lock lid; close pressure-release valve. Adjust to pressure-cook on low for 1 hour and 5 minutes. When finished cooking, quick-release pressure. The cheesecake should be jiggly but set in center.

5. Remove springform pan from pressure cooker; remove foil. Cool cheesecake on a wire rack 1 hour. Loosen sides from pan with a knife. Refrigerate overnight, covering when completely cooled.

6. For topping, melt chocolate and cream in a microwave; stir until smooth. Cool slightly. Remove rim from springform pan. Pour chocolate mixture over cheesecake. If desired, arrange kiwi slices into roses. Top cheesecake with kiwi and sprinkle with berries.

1 piece: 484 cal., 34g fat (19g sat. fat), 151mg chol., 357mg sod., 39g carb. (31g sugars, 0 fiber), 8g pro.

CHERRY & SPICE RICE PUDDING

Traverse City is called the cherry capital of the world. What better way to celebrate our orchards than by using plump, tart dried cherries in my favorite desserts?

—Deb Perry, Traverse City, MI

TAKES: 20 MIN. • MAKES: 12 SERVINGS

- 4 cups cooked rice
- 1 can (12 oz.) evaporated milk
- 1 cup 2% milk
- ⅓ cup sugar
- ¼ cup water
- ¾ cup dried cherries
- 3 Tbsp. butter, softened
- 2 tsp. vanilla extract
- ½ tsp. ground cinnamon
- ¼ tsp. ground nutmeg

1. Generously grease a 6-qt. electric pressure cooker. Add rice, milks, sugar and water; stir to combine. Stir in remaining ingredients.

2. Lock lid; close pressure-release valve. Adjust to pressure-cook on high for 3 minutes. Allow pressure to naturally release for 5 minutes, then quick-release any remaining pressure. Stir lightly. Serve warm or cold. Refrigerate leftovers.

1 serving: 202 cal., 6g fat (4g sat. fat), 19mg chol., 64mg sod., 33g carb. (16g sugars, 1g fiber), 4g pro.

CHOCOLATE-APRICOT DUMP CAKE

Years ago, I prepared a dessert similar to this in the oven. I converted it to my pressure cooker and now we can enjoy it quickly. Try it with white cake mix and blueberry pie filling.

—Joan Hallford, North Richland Hills, TX

PREP: 10 MIN. • COOK: 35 MIN. + STANDING • MAKES: 8 SERVINGS

- 1 can (21 oz.) apricot or peach pie filling
- 2 cups devil's food cake mix
- ½ cup chopped pecans, toasted
- ½ cup miniature semisweet chocolate chips, optional
- ½ cup butter, cubed
- Vanilla ice cream, optional

1. Place trivet insert and 1 cup water in a 6-qt. electric pressure cooker. Spread pie filling in the bottom of a greased 1½-qt. baking dish. Sprinkle with cake mix, pecans and if desired, chocolate chips. Dot with butter. Cover baking dish with foil.

2. Fold an 18x12-in. piece of foil lengthwise into thirds, making a sling. Use sling to lower the dish onto trivet. Lock lid; close pressure-release valve. Adjust to pressure-cook on high for 35 minutes. Quick-release pressure. Press cancel. Using foil sling, carefully remove baking dish. Let stand 10 minutes. If desired, serve warm cake with ice cream.

1 serving: 360 cal., 18g fat (9g sat. fat), 31mg chol., 436mg sod., 49g carb. (26g sugars, 1g fiber), 2g pro.

CHERRY & SPICE RICE PUDDING

MAPLE CREME BRULEE

MAPLE CREME BRULEE

The electric pressure cooker is the perfect cooking vessel for classic creme brulee. The crunchy brown sugar topping is wonderful, and the custard is smooth and creamy.
—Taste of Home *Test Kitchen*

PREP: 20 MIN. + CHILLING • COOK: 10 MIN. + RELEASING • MAKES: 3 SERVINGS

- 1⅓ cups heavy whipping cream
- 3 large egg yolks
- ½ cup packed brown sugar
- ¼ tsp. ground cinnamon
- ½ tsp. maple flavoring
- 1 cup water

TOPPING

- 1½ tsp. sugar
- 1½ tsp. brown sugar

1. Select saute setting on a 6-qt. electric pressure cooker and adjust for low heat. Add cream. Heat until bubbles form around sides of cooker. In a small bowl, whisk egg yolks, brown sugar and cinnamon. Press cancel; stir a small amount of hot cream into egg mixture. Return all to pressure cooker, stirring constantly. Stir in maple flavoring.

2. Transfer cream mixture to 3 greased 6-oz. ramekins or custard cups. Wipe pressure cooker clean. Pour in water; place trivet insert in bottom. Place ramekins on trivet, offset stacking as needed, and loosely cover with foil to prevent moisture from getting into ramekins. Lock lid; close pressure-release valve. Adjust to pressure-cook on high for 11 minutes.

3. When finished cooking, allow pressure to naturally release for 10 minutes, then quick-release any remaining pressure. A knife inserted in center should come out clean, though center will still be soft. Using tongs, remove the ramekins. Cool for 10 minutes; refrigerate, covered, for at least 4 hours.

4. For topping, combine sugars and sprinkle over ramekins. Hold a kitchen torch about 2 in. above custard surface; rotate slowly until sugar is evenly caramelized. Serve immediately.

1 serving: 578 cal., 44g fat (26g sat. fat), 350mg chol., 63mg sod., 44g carb. (40g sugars, 0 fiber), 5g pro.

TEST KITCHEN TIP: If you don't have a kitchen torch, you can brown these under the broiler. Preheat the broiler and place ramekins on a baking sheet; let stand at room temperature for 15 minutes. Broil 8 in. from heat until sugar is caramelized, 3-5 minutes. Refrigerate until firm, 1-2 hours.

SWEET & SOUR PINEAPPLE PORK, PAGE 181

AIR FRYER

French fries, popcorn shrimp and egg rolls are just the beginning. You can also use the handy air fryer to roast a veggie side dish for a family dinner or bake up a little treat to cure a sweet craving anytime.

AIR FRYER 101

Get ready for crispy french fries, onion rings, chicken wings and more fun foods without the mess or excess fat of deep-frying! Here's how to get started with your air fryer.

Start by checking the temperature. Just like with full-size ovens, temperatures may vary among air-fryer models. Test your air fryer to see if it runs above or below the selected temperature setting.

Know your air fryer's cooking times for the foods you make most regularly. Since air-fryer temperatures vary, so do cook times. That's why the air-fryer recipes in this book have wider time ranges. Determining your air fryer's ideal cooking times may take some trial and error at first. Check the food at the shortest cook time. If it's not done, check back a little later.

Give the food a shake (or a flip). To help food crisp, it's good practice to turn, rotate or shake contents in the air-fryer basket (just like flipping french fries, fish fillets or chicken strips when cooking in a traditional oven).

Cook food in a single layer for best results. Allow plenty of air circulation to get even cooking and crispy results. One exception in which you can stack and pack foods is if you're roasting veggies. For instance, load up your air-fryer basket with a pound of Brussels sprouts and roast them at 350° for 12-15 minutes, stirring once.

Always use a thermometer when cooking meat. Food can brown nicely on the outside before reaching its appropriate internal temperature, so check it with a thermometer to be sure it's safe to eat. The same goes for both fresh and previously frozen foods.

Bake up a little treat. Yes, you can bake homemade cookies—and other treats—in the air fryer! All it takes is a few minutes and chilled dough on standby. Models differ in their baking functions, so test just 1 or 2 cookies first. You may need to adjust the temperature or cooking time.

Take advantage of your air fryer when cooking for 1 or 2 people. Air fryers are small, making them great when you're cooking a low-yield meal. Any more than that, and you may have to cook in separate batches.

Seeing smoke? Don't panic. Unplug the air fryer and remove the food basket. Make sure no food is lodged in the heating coil. Return the food to the air fryer and continue cooking. If smoke persists, oil or residue may be on the heating element. Unplug the machine, cool, and then wipe the coil clean with a damp cloth, just like the heating coil on an electric stove. In the future, make sure to clean your air fryer regularly.

WHAT OUR TESTING REVEALED

Our Test Kitchen tested a variety of recipes using 6 different air-fryer models.

We discovered cook times can vary dramatically across different brands.

To accommodate this variance, the recipes in this book have a wider than normal range of suggested cook times. Begin checking the food at the first time listed in the recipe and adjust as needed.

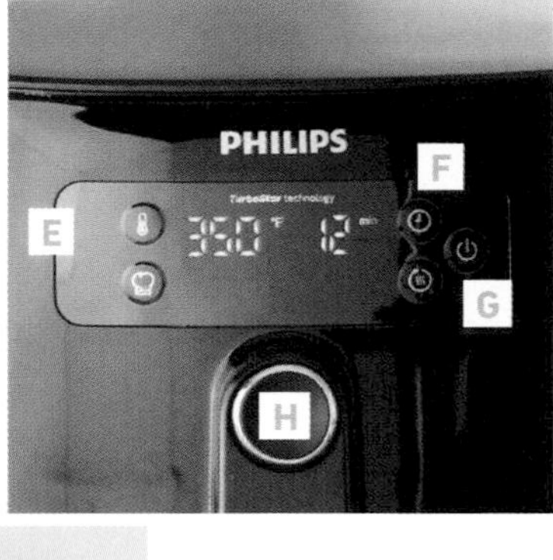

A. Heating coil (shown in last photo below)
B. Fan (inside unit)
C. Basket
D. Maximum fill line
E. Temperature setting
F. Time setting
G. Power
H. Basket release

CLEANING TIPS

- **Basket:** The basket, its holder and any dividing compartments that came with your air fryer are dishwasher safe. After each use, allow the air fryer to cool completely. Remove the cooled basket, tray and pan, and wash them as you would any other dish.
- **Exterior:** When it comes to cleaning the outside of an air fryer, a simple soapy wipe-down will do. Unplug the appliance and gently wipe with a damp cloth. That's it!
- **Heating Coil:** If oil or residue is on the heating coil, let the unplugged machine cool, then wipe the coil with a damp cloth—just as you would with the heating element on an electric stove.
- **Unexpected Mess?** If your cooking project was a bit messier than usual or the machine has developed an odd odor, your air fryer may require a deeper cleaning.

FIVE COMMON AIR-FRYER MISTAKES

They promise extra-crispy foods that are lower in fat, but if you don't use your air fryer properly, results may be less than dazzling.

Too much stuff on the counter. Air fyers rely on a constant flow of air to move the high-temperature heat around the food for all-over crispness, so make sure to keep at least 5 inches of clear space on all sides.

Not preheating the air fryer. Like an oven, an air fryer needs to be hot. If it's too cold, the final food may suffer. Check your recipe's suggested temperature before getting started.

Using too much or too little oil. Oil is a great medium to transfer heat. Most air fryer recipes call for only a teaspoon or 2 of oil. Refer to your recipe for the recommended amount for that dish, but when in doubt, give your food a quick spritz—just don't overdo it.

The foods are too wet. Don't put limp, wet veggies in an air fryer, as they will not crisp up properly. Instead, use your air fryer to quickly crisp already breaded or crunchy foods.

The food is too small. Food that is too small could slip through the slots in the air-fryer basket and fall onto a heating element. The pieces will burn quickly, which could result in fumes and smoke. It's best to keep your ingredients about the size of a Brussels sprout.

SNACKS

BUFFALO BITES WITH BLUE CHEESE RANCH DIP, PAGE 132

SHRIMP CAKE SLIDERS

SHRIMP CAKE SLIDERS

My family loves these shrimp sliders. The slaw dressing and shrimp cake patties can be made ahead. When you're ready to serve, toss the cabbage slaw, air-fry the shrimp cakes, assemble and enjoy.

—Kim Banick, Turner, OR

PREP: 30 MIN. + CHILLING • COOK: 10 MIN./BATCH • MAKES: 12 SLIDERS

- 1 lb. uncooked shrimp (41-50 per lb.), peeled and deveined
- 1 large egg, lightly beaten
- ½ cup finely chopped sweet red pepper
- 6 green onions, chopped and divided
- 1 Tbsp. minced fresh gingerroot
- ¼ tsp. salt
- 1 cup panko bread crumbs
- ¼ cup mayonnaise
- 1 Tbsp. Sriracha chili sauce
- 1 Tbsp. sweet chili sauce
- 5 cups shredded Chinese or napa cabbage
- 12 mini buns or dinner rolls, toasted
- 3 Tbsp. canola oil
- Additional Sriracha chili sauce, optional

1. Place shrimp in a food processor; pulse until chopped. In a large bowl, combine egg, red pepper, 4 green onions, ginger and salt. Add shrimp and bread crumbs; mix gently. Shape into twelve ½-in.-thick patties. Refrigerate 20 minutes.

2. Meanwhile, in a large bowl, combine mayonnaise and the chili sauces; stir in cabbage and remaining green onions.

3. Preheat air fryer to 375°. In batches, place patties in a single layer on greased tray in air-fryer basket. Cook until golden brown, 8-10 minutes. Serve on buns with slaw; secure with toothpicks. If desired, serve with additional chili sauce.

1 slider: 210 cal., 10g fat (1g sat. fat), 63mg chol., 321mg sod., 20g carb. (3g sugars, 1g fiber), 11g pro.

FIG & GOAT CHEESE MEATBALLS

Around the holidays, saucy cocktail meatballs are always the first appetizer to be eaten. In this dish, the sweet flavor of the fig glaze goes perfectly with pork and tangy goat cheese.
—Kim Banick, Turner, OR

PREP: 45 MIN. • COOK: 25 MIN. • MAKES: 1½ DOZEN

AIR FRYER

- ½ cup panko bread crumbs
- 1 large egg, lightly beaten
- 1 lb. bulk Italian sausage
- 2 oz. fresh goat cheese
- ½ cup red wine vinegar
- ¼ cup sugar
- 1 cinnamon stick (3 in.)
- 2 whole cloves
- 1 whole star anise
- ½ cup dried figs, chopped
- ½ cup water
- Chopped fresh chives, optional

1. Preheat air fryer to 350°. In a large bowl, combine bread crumbs and eggs. Add sausage; mix lightly but thoroughly. Divide into 18 portions. Shape each portion around ½ tsp. goat cheese to cover completely. in batches, place the meatballs on a greased tray in air-fryer basket. Cook until cooked through, 25-30 minutes.

2. Meanwhile, in a large saucepan, bring vinegar, sugar, cinnamon, cloves and star anise to a boil. Reduce heat; simmer 5 minutes. Discard cinnamon, cloves and star anise. Add figs; cook until softened, 8-10 minutes. Remove from heat; cool slightly. Transfer to a blender. Add ½ cup water; process until almost smooth. Serve with meatballs. If desired, top meatballs with chopped chives.

Freeze option: Freeze cooled meatballs and sauce in freezer containers. To use, partially thaw in refrigerator overnight. Heat through in a covered saucepan, stirring gently; add a little water if necessary.

1 meatball: 97 cal., 6g fat (2g sat. fat), 26mg chol., 175mg sod., 7g carb. (5g sugars, 0 fiber), 4g pro.

FIG & GOAT CHEESE
MEATBALLS
AIR
FRYER

SAMOSAS

SAMOSAS

Samosas are one of my family's absolute favorites. These crispy dough pockets are stuffed with potatoes and peas and then air-fried to give them a healthier twist. They'd make a perfect starter, side dish or buffet food for your next party.

—Soniya Saluja, Chantilly, VA

PREP: 20 MIN. + RISING • COOK: 15 MIN. • MAKES: 1 DOZEN

AIR FRYER

- 2 cups all-purpose flour
- 3 Tbsp. ghee or canola oil
- ½ tsp. salt
- ½ tsp. caraway seeds
- ¾ cup cold water

FILLING

- 5 medium potatoes, peeled and chopped
- 6 Tbsp. canola oil, divided
- 1 cup fresh or frozen peas, thawed
- 1 tsp. minced fresh gingerroot
- 1 tsp. garam masala
- ½ tsp. cumin seeds
- ½ tsp. salt
- Optional: Fennel seed, crushed coriander seeds, caraway seeds or amchur (dried mango powder)

1. In a large bowl, combine flour, ghee, salt and caraway seeds until mixture resembles bread crumbs. Gradually stir in enough cold water to form a firm dough. Turn onto a lightly floured surface; knead until smooth and elastic, 6-8 minutes. Cover and let rest for 1 hour.

2. Place potatoes in a large saucepan and cover with water. Bring to a boil. Reduce heat and cook until just tender, 8-10 minutes; drain. Set aside to cool slightly. In a large skillet, heat 3 Tbsp. oil over medium heat. Add potatoes and cook until potatoes start to cling to the skillet, about 5 minutes. Stir in peas, ginger, garam masala, cumin seeds and salt; cook until heated through, about 2 minutes. Stir in optional ingredients as desired. Set aside.

3. Divide dough into 6 pieces. Roll 1 piece of dough into a 10x6-in. oval. Cut dough in half. Moisten straight edge with water. Bring 1 corner of half moon up to meet other corner of the half moon, forming a cone. Pinch seam to seal. Fill with 3-4 Tbsp. potato mixture. Moisten curved edge of dough with water; fold over top of filling and and press seam to seal. Gently press bottom of samosa to flatten slightly. Repeat with remaining dough and filling.

4. Preheat air fryer to 350°. Brush samosas with remaining 3 Tbsp. oil. In batches, arrange in a single layer without touching in the air-fryer basket. Cook until golden brown, about 15 minutes.

1 samosa: 280 cal., 14g fat (3g sat. fat), 10mg chol., 203mg sod., 33g carb. (1g sugars, 3g fiber), 5g pro.

EGG ROLLS

My mom taught me how to make homemade egg rolls. Ever since she passed away, I think of her every time I make them. These taste so good, you'll never want a fast-food version again.

—Jenniffer Love, South Waltham, MA

PREP: 20 MIN. • COOK: 15 MIN./BATCH • MAKES: 18 SERVINGS

AIR FRYER

- 2 cups hot water
- 3 cups fresh bean sprouts
- 1 lb. ground chicken
- 6 green onions, chopped
- 1 Tbsp. minced fresh gingerroot
- 3 garlic cloves, minced
- 1 jar (11 oz.) Chinese-style sauce or duck sauce, divided
- 1 Tbsp. fish sauce or soy sauce
- 1 tsp. soy sauce
- 1 pkg. (14 oz.) coleslaw mix
- 1 pkg. (10 oz.) frozen chopped spinach, thawed and squeezed dry
- 18 egg roll wrappers

1. Pour hot water over bean sprouts in a small bowl; let stand 5 minutes. Drain.

2. Meanwhile, in a Dutch oven, cook the chicken over medium heat until no longer pink, 6-8 minutes, breaking into crumbles. Add green onions, ginger and garlic. Cook 1 minute longer; drain. Stir in ½ cup Chinese-style sauce, fish sauce and soy sauce; transfer to a large bowl. Wipe pan clean.

3. In same pan, cook and stir coleslaw mix, spinach and drained bean sprouts until crisp-tender, 4-5 minutes. Stir into chicken mixture. Cool slightly.

4. Preheat air fryer to 400°. With 1 corner of an egg roll wrapper facing you, place ⅓ cup filling just below center of wrapper. (Cover remaining wrappers with a damp paper towel until ready to use.) Fold bottom corner over filling; moisten remaining wrapper edges with water. Fold side corners toward center over filling. Roll egg roll up tightly, pressing at tip to seal. Repeat.

5. In batches, arrange egg rolls in a single layer in greased air-fryer basket; spritz with cooking spray. Cook until golden brown, 8-12 minutes. Turn; spritz with additional cooking spray. Cook golden brown, 4-6 minutes longer. Serve with remaining Chinese-style sauce.

1 egg roll: 187 cal., 3g fat (1g sat. fat), 20mg chol., 388mg sod., 33g carb. (7g sugars, 2g fiber), 9g pro.

EGG ROLLS

CINNAMON ALMONDS

CINNAMON ALMONDS

These crunchy cinnamon almonds are a spectacular treat to take to a party or gathering. They taste just like the roasted almonds you get at the fair.
—*Janice Thompson, Stacy, MN*

PREP: 15 MIN. • COOK: 25 MIN. + COOLING • MAKES: ABOUT 2CUPS

AIR FRYER

- 1 large egg white
- 1 Tbsp. vanilla extract
- 2 cups unblanched almonds
- 3 Tbsp. sugar
- 3 Tbsp. packed brown sugar
- ½ tsp. salt
- ½ tsp. ground cinnamon

1. Preheat air fryer to 300°. In a large bowl, beat egg white until frothy; beat in vanilla. Add the almonds; stir gently to coat. Combine the sugars, salt and cinnamon; add to nut mixture and stir gently to coat.

2. Arrange almonds in a single layer on greased tray in air-fryer basket. Cook until almonds are crisp, stirring once, 25-30 minutes. Cool. Store in an airtight container.

¼ cup: 254 cal., 19g fat (1g sat. fat), 0 chol., 163mg sod., 16g carb. (11g sugars, 4g fiber), 8g pro.

BLOODY MARY DEVILED EGGS

Take the guesswork out of cooking hard-boiled eggs by making them in an air fryer. Then give them a unique Bloody Mary-inspired spin.
—Taste of Home *Test Kitchen*

PREP: 20 MIN. • COOK: 15 MIN. + CHILLING • MAKES: 1 DOZEN

- 6 large eggs
- 3 Tbsp. reduced-fat mayonnaise
- 1 Tbsp. reduced-sodium tomato juice
- ¾ tsp. prepared horseradish
- ¼ tsp. hot pepper sauce
- ⅛ tsp. salt
- ⅛ tsp. pepper
- Crumbled cooked bacon, optional

1. Preheat air-fryer to 275°. Place eggs in a single layer on tray in air-fryer basket. Cook 15 minutes. Remove eggs; rinse in cold water and place in ice water until completely cooled. Remove shells; cut eggs in half lengthwise. Remove yolks; set aside egg whites and 4 yolks (discard remaining yolks or save for another use).

2. In a large bowl, mash reserved yolks. Stir in mayonnaise, tomato juice, horseradish, pepper sauce, salt and pepper. Stuff or pipe into egg whites. If desired, garnish with bacon. Chill until serving.

1 stuffed egg half: 40 cal., 3g fat (1g sat. fat), 63mg chol., 81mg sod., 1g carb. (0 sugars, 0 fiber), 3g pro.

AIR FRYER

BACON-WRAPPED AVOCADO WEDGES

Almost everything is better with bacon, and avocado is no exception. Since this appetizer is made in an air fryer, it bakes up crispy and fast. It will definitely impress your friends!

—James Schend, Pleasant Prairie, WI

TAKES: 30 MIN. • MAKES: 1 DOZEN

- 2 medium ripe avocados
- 12 bacon strips

SAUCE

- ½ cup mayonnaise
- 2 to 3 Tbsp. Sriracha chili sauce
- 1 to 2 Tbsp. lime juice
- 1 tsp. grated lime zest

1. Preheat air fryer to 400°. Cut each avocado in half; remove pit and peel. Cut each half into thirds. Wrap 1 bacon slice around each avocado wedge. Working in batches if needed, place wedges in a single layer in fryer basket and cook until bacon is cooked through, 10-15 minutes.

2. Meanwhile, in a small bowl, stir together mayonnaise, chili sauce, lime juice and zest. Serve wedges with sauce.

1 wedge: 142 cal., 13g fat (3g sat. fat), 9mg chol., 274mg sod., 3g carb. (1g sugars, 2g fiber), 3g pro.

BACON-WRAPPED
AVOCADO WEDGES

CHILI-LIME CHICKPEAS

CHILI-LIME CHICKPEAS

Looking for a lighter snack that's still a crowd pleaser? You've found it! These zesty, crunchy chickpeas will have everyone happily munching.

—Julie Ruble, Charlotte, NC

PREP: 10 MIN. • BAKE: 40 MIN. + COOLING • MAKES: 1 CUP

AIR FRYER

- 1 can (15 oz.) chickpeas or garbanzo beans, rinsed, drained and patted dry
- 1 Tbsp. extra virgin olive oil
- 1½ tsp. chili powder
- 1 tsp. ground cumin
- ½ tsp. grated lime zest
- 1½ tsp. lime juice
- ¼ tsp. sea salt

1. Preheat air fryer to 400°. Spread chickpeas in a single layer on greased tray in air-fryer basket, removing any loose skins. Cook until very crunchy, 20-30 minutes, shaking basket every 5 minutes.

2. Meanwhile, whisk together remaining ingredients. Remove chickpeas from air fryer; let cool 5 minutes. Drizzle with oil mixture; toss to coat. Cool completely before serving.

¼ cup: 133 cal., 6g fat (0 sat. fat), 0 chol., 287mg sod., 17g carb. (3g sugars, 5g fiber), 4g pro.

WHY YOU'LL LOVE IT...

"My new favorite snack! The lime gives it the tiniest hint of sweetness."

—LISASPRIGGS, TASTEOFHOME.COM

BUFFALO BITES WITH BLUE CHEESE RANCH DIP

Low-carb cauliflower bites cook up fast in the air fryer, making them an easy snack or side dish. I serve them with a flavorful dip that's packed with protein. My teenagers happily eat their veggies with this recipe.
—Julie Peterson, Crofton, MD

AIR FRYER

PREP: 10 MIN. • COOK: 30 MIN. • MAKES: 6 SERVINGS

- 1 small head cauliflower, cut into florets
- 2 Tbsp. olive oil
- 3 Tbsp. butter, melted
- 3 Tbsp. Buffalo wing sauce

DIP

- 1½ cups 2% cottage cheese
- ¼ cup fat-free plain Greek yogurt
- ¼ cup crumbled blue cheese
- 1 envelope ranch salad dressing mix
- Celery sticks, optional

1. Preheat air fryer to 350°. In a large bowl, combine cauliflower and oil; toss to coat. In batches, arrange cauliflower in a single layer in air-fryer basket. Cook until florets are tender and edges are browned, 10-15 minutes, stirring halfway through.

2. In a large bowl, combine buffalo sauce and melted butter. Add cauliflower; toss to coat. Transfer to a serving platter. In a small bowl, combine the dip ingredients. Serve with cauliflower and, if desired, celery sticks.

1 serving: 203 cal., 13g fat (6g sat. fat), 22mg chol., 1470mg sod., 13g carb. (4g sugars, 1g fiber), 8g pro.

BUFFALO BITES WITH BLUE CHEESE RANCH DIP

ZUCCHINI PIZZA FRITTERS

ZUCCHINI PIZZA FRITTERS

These zucchini pizza fritters are the perfect after-school snack. They're also freezer friendly, so you can make a batch or two to enjoy later.

—Marissa Allen, Frisco, TX

PREP: 20 MIN. • COOK: 15 MIN./BATCH • MAKES: 12 SERVINGS

AIR FRYER

- 2 medium zucchini
- 1 medium potato, peeled
- ½ small onion
- 1 large egg, lightly beaten
- 2 Tbsp. all-purpose flour
- ½ cup shredded Parmesan cheese
- 1 tsp. garlic powder
- 1 tsp. onion powder
- ½ tsp. dried parsley flakes
- ½ tsp. salt
- 1 tsp. pepper
- Optional: Marinara sauce, tzatziki sauce or ranch dressing

1. Preheat air fryer to 400°. Coarsely grate zucchini, potato and onion. Place grated vegetables on a double thickness of cheesecloth or a clean tea towel; bring up corners and squeeze out any liquid. Transfer to a large bowl; stir in egg, flour, Parmesan, garlic powder, onion powder, parsley, salt and pepper. Form mixture into ¼-cup patties.

2. In batches, place patties in a single layer onto greased tray in air-fryer basket. Cook until lightly browned, 15-20 minutes. Serve with sauce or dressing if desired.

1 fritter: 44 cal., 1g fat (1g sat. fat), 18mg chol., 164mg sod., 5g carb. (1g sugars, 1g fiber), 3g pro.

SIDES

BACON-PEANUT BUTTER CORNBREAD MUFFINS, PAGE 148

BEETS WITH ORANGE GREMOLATA & GOAT CHEESE

BEETS WITH ORANGE GREMOLATA & GOAT CHEESE

My grandma inspired my love of beets—she grew them in her garden and then pickled or canned them. I prepare mine in my air fryer with fresh herbs and tangy goat cheese. They're wonderful in winter, and also all year long.

—Courtney Archibeque, Greeley, CO

PREP: 25 MIN. • COOK: 45 MIN. + COOLING • MAKES: 12 SERVINGS

- 3 medium fresh golden beets (about 1 lb.)
- 3 medium fresh beets (about 1 lb.)
- 2 Tbsp. lime juice
- 2 Tbsp. orange juice
- ½ tsp. fine sea salt
- 1 Tbsp. minced fresh parsley
- 1 Tbsp. minced fresh sage
- 1 garlic clove, minced
- 1 tsp. grated orange zest
- 3 Tbsp. crumbled goat cheese
- 2 Tbsp. sunflower kernels

1. Preheat air fryer to 400°. Scrub beets and trim tops by 1 in. Place beets on a double thickness of heavy-duty foil (about 24x12 in.). Fold foil around beets, sealing tightly. Place in a single layer on tray in air-fryer basket. Cook until tender, 45-55 minutes. Open foil carefully to allow steam to escape.

2. When cool enough to handle, peel, halve and slice beets; place in a serving bowl. Add the lime juice, orange juice and salt; toss to coat. Combine parsley, sage, garlic and orange zest; sprinkle over beets. Top with goat cheese and sunflower kernels. Serve warm or chilled.

¾ cup: 49 cal., 1g fat (0 sat. fat), 2mg chol., 157mg sod., 9g carb. (6g sugars, 2g fiber), 2g pro.

CUMIN CARROTS

Carrots make a super side—big on flavor and a breeze to cook. Plus, I can actually get my husband to eat these fragrant, deeply spiced veggies.
—Taylor Kiser, Brandon, FL

PREP: 20 MIN. • COOK: 15 MIN. • MAKES: 4 SERVINGS

- 2 tsp. coriander seeds
- 2 tsp. cumin seeds
- 1 lb. carrots, peeled and cut into 4x½-in. sticks
- 1 Tbsp. melted coconut oil or butter
- 2 garlic cloves, minced
- ¼ tsp. salt
- ⅛ tsp. pepper
- Minced fresh cilantro, optional

1. Preheat air fryer to 325°. In a dry small skillet, toast coriander and cumin seeds over medium heat 45-60 seconds or until aromatic, stirring frequently. Cool slightly. Grind in a spice grinder, or with a mortar and pestle, until finely crushed.

2. Place carrots in a large bowl. Add melted coconut oil, garlic, salt, pepper and crushed spices; toss to coat. Place on greased tray in air-fryer basket.

3. Cook until crisp-tender and lightly browned, 12-15 minutes, stirring occasionally. If desired, sprinkle with cilantro.

1 serving: 86 cal., 4g fat (3g sat. fat), 0 chol., 228mg sod., 12g carb. (5g sugars, 4g fiber), 1g pro. **Diabetic exchanges:** 1 vegetable, 1 fat.

CUMIN CARROTS

HERB & LEMON
CAULIFLOWER

HERB & LEMON CAULIFLOWER

A standout cauliflower side dish is easy to prepare in the air fryer with just a few ingredients. Crushed red pepper flakes add a touch of heat.

—Susan Hein, Burlington, WI

TAKES: 20 MIN. • MAKES: 4 SERVINGS

- 1 medium head cauliflower, cut into florets (about 6 cups)
- 4 Tbsp. olive oil, divided
- ¼ cup minced fresh parsley
- 1 Tbsp. minced fresh rosemary
- 1 Tbsp. minced fresh thyme
- 1 tsp. grated lemon zest
- 2 Tbsp. lemon juice
- ½ tsp. salt
- ¼ tsp. crushed red pepper flakes

Preheat air fryer to 350°. In a large bowl, combine cauliflower and 2 Tbsp. olive, toss to coat. In batches, arrange cauliflower in a single layer on tray in air-fryer basket. Cook until florets are tender and edges are browned, 8-10 minutes, stirring halfway through. In a small bowl, combine remaining ingredients; stir in remaining 2 Tbsp. oil. Transfer cauliflower to a large bowl; drizzle with herb mixture and toss to combine.

¾ cup: 161 cal., 14g fat (2g sat. fat), 0 chol., 342mg sod., 8g carb. (3g sugars, 3g fiber), 3g pro. **Diabetic exchanges:** 3 fat, 1 vegetable.

QUINOA ARANCINI

We love arancini, but because these rice balls are typically fried in oil, they are not the healthiest snack around. I wanted to make a version we could enjoy guilt-free. I used quinoa instead of rice and baked them in the air fryer instead of deep frying. Now we can have them anytime.
—Sabrina Ovadia, New York, NY

TAKES: 25 MIN. • MAKES: 3 SERVINGS

AIR FRYER

- 1 pkg. (9 oz.) ready-to-serve quinoa or 1¾ cups cooked quinoa
- 2 large eggs, lightly beaten, divided use
- 1 cup seasoned bread crumbs, divided
- ¼ cup shredded Parmesan cheese
- 1 Tbsp. olive oil
- 2 Tbsp. minced fresh basil or 2 tsp. dried basil
- ½ tsp. garlic powder
- ½ tsp. salt
- ⅛ tsp. pepper
- 6 cubes part-skim mozzarella cheese (¾ in. each)
- Cooking spray
- Warmed pasta sauce, optional

1. Preheat air fryer to 375°. Prepare the quinoa according to the package directions. Stir in 1 egg, ½ cup bread crumbs, Parmesan cheese, olive oil, basil and seasonings.

2. Divide into 6 portions. Shape each portion around a cheese cube to cover completely, forming a ball.

3. Place the remaining egg and ½ cup bread crumbs in separate shallow bowls. Dip quinoa balls in egg, then roll in bread crumbs. Place on greased tray in air-fryer basket; spritz with cooking spray. Cook until golden brown, 6-8 minutes. If desired, serve with pasta sauce.

2 arancini: 423 cal., 19g fat (6g sat. fat), 142mg chol., 1283mg sod., 40g carb. (4g sugars, 5g fiber), 21g pro.

WHY YOU'LL LOVE IT...

"These were amazing! My husband said, 'Fabulous,' and he felt like he was at a restaurant! I doubled the recipe, and I'm glad I did. Easy to make and I like that they're baked and not fried."

—PATTIEJEAN, TASTEOFHOME.COM

QUINOA
ARANCINI

FRENCH FRIES

FRENCH FRIES

These low-calorie french fries are perfect because I can whip them up at a moment's notice with ingredients I have on hand. They are so crispy, you won't miss the deep fryer!
—Dawn Parker, Surrey, BC

PREP: 10 MIN. • COOK: 30 MIN. • MAKES: 4 SERVINGS

AIR FRYER

- 3 medium potatoes, cut into ½-in. strips
- 2 Tbsp. coconut or avocado oil
- ½ tsp. garlic powder
- ¼ tsp. salt
- ¼ tsp. pepper
- Chopped fresh parsley, optional

1. Preheat air fryer to 400°. Add potatoes to a large bowl; add enough ice water to cover. Soak for 15 minutes. Drain potatoes; place on towels and pat dry.

2. Combine potatoes, oil, garlic powder, salt and pepper in second large bowl; toss to coat. In batches, place potatoes in a single layer on tray in greased air-fryer basket. Cook until crisp and golden brown, 15-17 minutes, stirring and turning every 5-7 minutes. If desired, sprinkle with parsley.

¾ cup: 185 cal., 7g fat (6g sat. fat), 0 chol., 157mg sod., 28g carb. (1g sugars, 3g fiber), 3g pro. **Diabetic exchanges:** 2 starch, 1½ fat.

BACON-PEANUT BUTTER CORNBREAD MUFFINS

My family just can't get enough bacon and peanut butter, so I created these quick and easy cornbread muffins using ingredients I regularly keep stocked in my pantry and fridge. The streusel topping adds a delicious sweet-salty crunch. For a different flavor twist, swap in chocolate chips, then drizzle the warm muffins with chocolate syrup instead of caramel.

—Shannon Kohn, Summerville, SC

PREP: 25 MIN. • COOK: 20 MIN. • MAKES: 6 MUFFINS

- 6 Tbsp. softened butter, divided
- ½ cup dry roasted peanuts, chopped
- 1 pkg. (2.1 oz.) ready-to-serve fully cooked bacon, finely chopped, divided
- 1 Tbsp. light brown sugar
- 1 pkg. (8½ oz.) cornbread/muffin mix
- ½ cup buttermilk
- 2 large eggs, room temperature
- ¼ cup creamy peanut butter
- ⅔ cup peanut butter chips
- Caramel ice cream topping, optional

1. Preheat air fryer to 375°. Grease six 6-oz. ramekins with 2 Tbsp. butter. For topping, in a small bowl combine 2 Tbsp. butter, peanuts, 3 Tbsp. bacon and brown sugar; set aside.

2. In a large bowl, beat muffin mix, buttermilk and eggs. Microwave peanut butter and remaining 2 Tbsp. butter until melted; stir into batter. Fold in the peanut butter chips and remaining ⅔ cup bacon. Pour batter into prepared ramekins; sprinkle with topping.

3. Place ramekins on tray in air-fryer basket; cook until a toothpick inserted in center comes out clean, 20-25 minutes. Cool 5 minutes before removing ramekins from air fryer to a wire rack. Serve warm. If desired, drizzle with caramel ice cream topping.

1 muffin: 590 cal., 38g fat (15g sat. fat), 94mg chol., 818mg sod., 45g carb. (20g sugars, 5g fiber), 18g pro.

BACON-PEANUT BUTTER CORNBREAD MUFFINS

ROASTED GREEN BEANS

ROASTED GREEN BEANS

Our family loves roasted green beans, but they can take a long time in the oven. I tested these in our air fryer. They cooked in less time and we loved them!

—Courtney Stultz, Weir, KS

PREP: 15 MIN. • COOK: 20 MIN. • MAKES: 6 SERVINGS

AIR FRYER

- 1 lb. fresh green beans, cut into 2 in. pieces
- ½ lb. sliced fresh mushrooms
- 1 small red onion, halved and thinly sliced
- 2 Tbsp. olive oil
- 1 tsp. Italian seasoning
- ¼ tsp. salt
- ⅛ tsp. pepper

1. Preheat air fryer to 375°. In a large bowl, combine all ingredients; toss to coat.

2. Arrange the vegetables on greased tray in air-fryer basket. Cook until just tender, 8-10 minutes. Toss beans to redistribute; cook until browned, 8-10 minutes longer.

⅔ cup: 76 cal., 5g fat (1g sat. fat), 0 chol., 105mg sod., 8g carb. (3g sugars, 3g fiber), 3g pro. **Diabetic exchanges:** 1 vegetable, 1 fat.

RADISHES

Radishes aren't just for salads anymore. When cooked in the air fryer, this abundant springtime veggie makes a colorful side dish for any meal.
—Taste of Home *Test Kitchen*

TAKES: 25 MIN. • MAKES: 6 SERVINGS

AIR FRYER

- 2¼ lbs. radishes, trimmed and quartered (about 6 cups)
- 3 Tbsp. olive oil
- 1 Tbsp. minced fresh oregano or 1 tsp. dried oregano
- ¼ tsp. salt
- ⅛ tsp. pepper

Preheat air fryer to 375°. Toss radishes with remaining ingredients. In batches, place radishes on greased tray in air-fryer basket. Cook until crisp-tender, 12-15 minutes, stirring occasionally.

⅔ cup: 88 cal., 7g fat (1g sat. fat), 0 chol., 165mg sod., 6g carb. (3g sugars, 3g fiber), 1g pro. **Diabetic exchanges:** 1½ fat, 1 vegetable.

RADISHES

PARMESAN BREADED SQUASH

PARMESAN BREADED SQUASH

Baked yellow squash is beautifully crispy when cooked in the air fryer. You don't have to turn the pieces, but do keep an eye on them.
—Debi Mitchell, Flower Mound, TX

PREP: 15 MIN. • COOK: 30 MIN./BATCH • MAKES: 4 SERVINGS

AIR FRYER

- 4 cups thinly sliced yellow summer squash (3 medium)
- 3 Tbsp. olive oil
- ½ tsp. salt
- ½ tsp. pepper
- ⅛ tsp. cayenne pepper
- ¾ cup panko bread crumbs
- ¾ cup grated Parmesan cheese

1. Preheat air fryer to 350°. Place squash in a large bowl. Add the oil and seasonings; toss to coat.

2. In a shallow bowl, mix bread crumbs and cheese. Dip squash in crumb mixture to coat both sides, patting to help coating adhere. In batches, arrange squash in a single layer on tray in air-fryer basket. Cook until squash is tender and the coating is golden brown, about 10 minutes.

½ cup: 203 cal., 14g fat (3g sat. fat), 11mg chol., 554mg sod., 13g carb. (4g sugars, 2g fiber), 6g pro. **Diabetic exchanges:** 3 fat, 1 vegetable, ½ starch.

WHY YOU'LL LOVE IT...

"Phenomenal! I am not a squash fan, but I love this recipe—it gives the squash great flavor and texture. I bake mine a little longer because I like them crispy!"

—MAMATRICIA, TASTEOFHOME.COM

RED POTATOES

These red potatoes are simple to prepare in the air fryer, yet elegant in color and flavor. Fragrant rosemary, fresh or dried, gives this side dish a distinctive but subtle taste.
—Margie Wampler, Butler, PA

TAKES: 20 MIN. • MAKES: 8 SERVINGS

- 2 lbs. small unpeeled red potatoes, cut into wedges
- 2 Tbsp. olive oil
- 1 Tbsp. minced fresh rosemary or 1 tsp. dried rosemary, crushed
- 2 garlic cloves, minced
- ½ tsp. salt
- ¼ tsp. pepper

1. Preheat air fryer to 400°. Drizzle potatoes with oil. Sprinkle with rosemary, garlic salt and pepper; toss gently to coat.

2. Place on ungreased tray in air-fryer basket. Cook until potatoes are golden brown and tender, 10-12 minutes, stirring once.

1 cup: 113 cal., 4g fat (0 sat. fat), 0 chol., 155mg sod., 18g carb. (1g sugars, 2g fiber), 2g pro. **Diabetic exchanges:** 1 starch, 1 fat.

RED POTATOES

ENTREES

ROSEMARY-LEMON CHICKEN THIGHS, PAGE 186

POPCORN SHRIMP TACOS WITH CABBAGE SLAW

POPCORN SHRIMP TACOS WITH CABBAGE SLAW

I love combining classic flavors in new ways. This healthy recipe combines crispy popcorn shrimp and tacos. It's one of my family's favorites. To make them lower in carbs, use lettuce instead of tortillas.

—Julie Peterson, Crofton, MD

TAKES: 30 MIN. • MAKES: 4 SERVINGS

- 2 cups coleslaw mix
- ¼ cup minced fresh cilantro
- 2 Tbsp. lime juice
- 2 Tbsp. honey
- ¼ tsp. salt
- 1 jalapeno pepper, seeded and minced, optional
- 2 large eggs
- 2 Tbsp. 2% milk
- ½ cup all-purpose flour
- 1½ cups panko bread crumbs
- 1 Tbsp. ground cumin
- 1 Tbsp. garlic powder
- 1 lb. uncooked shrimp (41-50 per lb.), peeled and deveined
- Cooking spray
- 8 corn tortillas (6 in.), warmed
- 1 medium ripe avocado, peeled and sliced

1. In a small bowl, combine coleslaw mix, cilantro, lime juice, honey, salt and, if desired, jalapeno; toss to coat. Set aside.

2. Preheat air fryer to 375°. In a shallow bowl, whisk eggs and milk. Place flour in a separate shallow bowl. In a third shallow bowl, mix panko, cumin and garlic powder. Dip shrimp in flour to coat both sides; shake off excess. Dip in egg mixture, then in panko mixture, patting to help coating adhere.

3. In batches, arrange shrimp in a single layer in greased air-fryer basket; spritz with cooking spray. Cook until golden brown, 2-3 minutes. Turn; spritz with cooking spray. Cook until other side is golden brown and shrimp turn pink, 2-3 minutes longer.

4. Serve shrimp in tortillas with coleslaw mix and avocado.

Note: Wear disposable gloves when cutting hot peppers; the oils can burn skin. Avoid touching your face.

2 tacos: 456 cal., 12g fat (2g sat. fat), 213mg chol., 414mg sod., 58g carb. (11g sugars, 8g fiber), 29g pro.

QUICK TATER TOTS BAKE

I prepare this comforting dish when I'm short on time. You can also assemble it in individual ramekins if you don't have a larger baking dish that fits in your air fryer.
—Jean Ferguson, Elverta, CA

PREP: 15 MIN. • COOK: 30 MIN. • MAKES: 4 SERVINGS

- ¾ to 1 lb. ground beef or turkey
- 1 small onion, chopped
- Salt and pepper to taste
- 1 pkg. (16 oz.) frozen Tater Tots
- 1 can (10¾ oz.) condensed cream of mushroom soup, undiluted
- ⅔ cup 2% milk or water
- 1 cup shredded cheddar cheese

1. Preheat air fryer to 350°. In a large skillet, cook the beef and onion over medium heat until meat is no longer pink; drain. Season with salt and pepper.

2. Transfer to a greased 2-qt. baking dish that will fit in the air-fryer basket. Top with Tater Tots. Combine soup and milk; pour over potatoes. Sprinkle with cheese. Place baking dish on tray in air-fryer basket. Cook, uncovered, until heated through, 30-40 minutes.

1½ cups: 570 cal., 35g fat (12g sat. fat), 87mg chol., 1357mg sod., 37g carb. (5g sugars, 4g fiber), 26g pro.

SESAME-GINGER SALMON

We like to eat healthy, and fish is one of our favorite proteins. I look for new and unique ways to prepare salmon so we can enjoy a variety of flavors. This dish always hits the spot.
—Jennifer Berry, Lexington, OH

PREP: 15 MIN. + MARINATING • COOK: 15 MIN. • MAKES: 4 SERVINGS

- 1 cup sesame ginger salad dressing, divided
- 4 green onions, chopped
- 2 Tbsp. minced fresh cilantro
- 4 salmon fillets (4 oz. each)

1. In a large bowl or shallow dish, combine ⅔ cup dressing, onions and cilantro. Add salmon and turn to coat. Refrigerate for 30 minutes.

2. Preheat air fryer to 375°. Drain salmon, discarding marinade. Place salmon in a single layer on greased tray in air-fryer basket.

3. Place baking dish on tray in air fryer. Cook for 10 minutes. Baste with remaining dressing. Cook until fish flakes easily with a fork, 5-10 minutes. Drizzle with pan juices before serving.

1 fillet: 234 cal., 15g fat (3g sat. fat), 57mg chol., 208mg sod., 4g carb. (3g sugars, 0 fiber), 19g pro.

QUICK TATER
TOTS BAKE

JAMAICAN BEEF PATTIES

JAMAICAN BEEF PATTIES

My mom was born in Jamaica and lived there until she moved to the United States during her university years. I've loved these beef patties for most of my life. The savory flavor and spices are just right, and the pastry is flaky and delicious.

—Natasha Watson, Douglasville, GA

PREP: 35 MIN. • COOK: 25 MIN. • MAKES: 8 SERVINGS

AIR FRYER

- 1 lb. ground beef
- 1 medium onion, chopped
- 1 tsp. curry powder
- 1 tsp. dried thyme
- 1 tsp. pepper
- ¾ tsp. salt

CRUST

- 2 cups all-purpose flour
- 1½ tsp. curry powder
- Dash salt
- ½ cup cold butter
- ⅓ cup ice water
- 1 large egg, lightly beaten

1. In a large skillet, cook beef and onion over medium heat until beef is no longer pink and onion is tender, 6-8 minutes, breaking up beef into crumbles; drain. Stir in curry powder, thyme, pepper and salt; set aside.

2. For crust, in a large bowl, whisk together flour, curry powder and salt. Cut in butter until mixture resembles coarse crumbs. Add water; stir just until moistened.

3. Preheat air fryer to 350°. Divide dough into 8 portions. On a lightly floured surface, roll each portion into a 6-in. circle. Place about ¼ cup filling on 1 half of each circle. Fold crust over filling. Press edges with a fork to seal.

4. In batches if necessary, place in a single layer on greased tray in air-fryer basket; brush with beaten egg. Cook until golden brown, 22-25 minutes. Remove to wire racks. Serve warm.

Freeze option: Cover and freeze unbaked pastries on a parchment-lined baking sheet until firm. Transfer to freezer containers; return to freezer. To use, cook pastries on a greased tray in air-fryer basket in a preheated 350° air fryer until heated through, 25-30 minutes.

1 patty: 336 cal., 19g fat (10g sat. fat), 89mg chol., 373mg sod., 26g carb. (1g sugars, 2g fiber), 14g pro.

BACON-BROCCOLI QUICHE CUPS

Chock-full of veggies and melted cheese, this colorful egg bake has become a holiday brunch classic. For a tasty variation, use asparagus in place of the broccoli and Swiss cheese instead of cheddar.
—Irene Steinmeyer, Denver, CO

TAKES: 30 MIN. • MAKES: 2 SERVINGS

- 4 bacon strips, chopped
- ¼ cup small fresh broccoli florets
- ¼ cup chopped onion
- 1 garlic clove, minced
- 3 large eggs
- 1 Tbsp. dried parsley flakes
- ⅛ tsp. seasoned salt
- Dash pepper
- ¼ cup shredded cheddar cheese
- 2 Tbsp. chopped tomato

1. Preheat air fryer to 400°. In a skillet, cook bacon over medium heat until crisp, stirring occasionally. Remove bacon with a slotted spoon; drain on paper towels. Pour off drippings, reserving 2 tsp. in pan.

2. Add broccoli and onion to drippings in pan; cook and stir 2-3 minutes or until tender. Add garlic; cook 1 minute longer.

3. In a small bowl, whisk eggs, parsley, seasoned salt and pepper until blended. Stir in cheese, tomato, bacon and broccoli mixture.

4. Divide mixture evenly between 2 greased 10-oz. ramekins or custard cups. Place ramekins on tray in air-fryer basket. Cook until a knife inserted in center comes out clean, 20-25 minutes.

1 serving: 301 cal., 23g fat (9g sat. fat), 314mg chol., 598mg sod., 5g carb. (2g sugars, 1g fiber), 19g pro.

WHY YOU'LL LOVE IT...

"My mom loves this recipe! It doesn't have the carbs that most quiches have, so she can eat it without feeling guilty."

—MALINROSE, TASTEOFHOME.COM

BACON-BROCCOLI QUICHE CUPS

RASPBERRY BALSAMIC SMOKED PORK CHOPS

RASPBERRY BALSAMIC SMOKED PORK CHOPS

Air-fried pork chops are so delicious and so easy to make. My husband loves them.
—Lynn Moretti, Oconomowoc, WI

TAKES: 30 MIN. • MAKES: 2 SERVINGS

- 1 large egg
- 2 Tbsp. 2% milk
- ½ cup panko bread crumbs
- ½ cup finely chopped pecans
- 2 smoked bone-in pork chops (7½ oz. each)
- 2 Tbsp. all-purpose flour
- Cooking spray
- 3 Tbsp. balsamic vinegar
- 1 Tbsp. brown sugar
- 1 Tbsp. seedless raspberry jam
- 1½ tsp. thawed frozen orange juice concentrate

1. Preheat air fryer to 400°. Spritz air-fryer basket with cooking spray. In a shallow bowl, whisk together egg and milk. In another shallow bowl, toss bread crumbs with pecans.

2. Coat pork chops with flour; shake off excess. Dip in egg mixture, then in crumb mixture, patting to help adhere. Place chops in single layer in air-fryer basket; spritz with cooking spray.

3. Cook until golden brown, 12-15 minutes, turning halfway through cooking and spritzing with additional cooking spray. Meanwhile, place remaining ingredients in a small saucepan; bring to a boil. Cook and stir until slightly thickened, 6-8 minutes. Serve with chops.

1 pork chop with 1 Tbsp. glaze: 560 cal., 34g fat (10g sat. fat), 103mg chol., 1369mg sod., 35g carb. (22g sugars, 2g fiber), 32g pro.

TEST KITCHEN TIP: If you can't find smoked pork chops or want a lower-sodium alternative, this recipe will work with fresh chops, too. Season the meat with salt and pepper before coating, and cook the chops to at least 145°.

TURKEY & MUSHROOM POTPIES

I use the leftovers from our big holiday turkey to prepare these mini potpies. I think my family enjoys them more than the original feast!

—Lily Julow, Lawrenceville, GA

PREP: 40 MIN. • COOK: 20 MIN. • MAKES: 8 SERVINGS

- 4⅓ cups sliced baby portobello mushrooms
- 1 large onion, chopped
- 1 Tbsp. olive oil
- 2½ cups cubed cooked turkey
- 1 pkg. (16 oz.) frozen peas and carrots
- ¼ tsp. salt
- ¼ tsp. pepper
- ¼ cup cornstarch
- 2½ cups chicken broth
- ¼ cup sour cream

TOPPING

- 1½ cups all-purpose flour
- 2 tsp. sugar
- 1½ tsp. baking powder
- 1 tsp. dried thyme
- ¼ tsp. baking soda
- ¼ tsp. salt
- 2 Tbsp. cold butter
- 1 cup buttermilk
- 1 Tbsp. canola oil

1. In a Dutch oven, cook mushrooms and onion in oil until tender. Stir in turkey, peas and carrots, salt and pepper. Combine cornstarch and broth until smooth; gradually stir into pan. Bring to a boil. Reduce heat; cook and stir 2 minutes or until thickened. Stir in sour cream. Transfer to 8 greased 8-oz. ramekins.

2. Preheat air fryer to 400°. In a large bowl, combine flour, sugar, baking powder, thyme, baking soda and salt. Cut in butter until mixture resembles coarse crumbs. In a small bowl, combine buttermilk and oil; stir into dry ingredients just until moistened. Drop by heaping teaspoonfuls over filling.

3. In batches if necessary, place ramekins on tray in air-fryer basket. Cook until topping is golden brown and filling is bubbly, 20-25 minutes. Let stand 5 minutes before serving.

1 serving: 308 cal., 11g fat (4g sat. fat), 56mg chol., 759mg sod., 34g carb. (5g sugars, 3g fiber), 20g pro.

TURKEY &
MUSHROOM POTPIES

SPINACH FETA TURNOVERS

SPINACH FETA TURNOVERS

These quick and easy turnovers are one of my wife's favorite entrees. The refrigerated pizza dough makes preparation a snap!

—David Baruch, Weston, FL

TAKES: 30 MIN. • MAKES: 4 SERVINGS

- 2 large eggs
- 1 pkg. (10 oz.) frozen leaf spinach, thawed, squeezed dry and chopped
- ¾ cup crumbled feta cheese
- 2 garlic cloves, minced
- ¼ tsp. pepper
- 1 tube (13.8 oz.) refrigerated pizza crust
- Refrigerated tzatziki sauce, optional

1. Preheat air fryer to 425°. In a bowl, whisk eggs; set aside 1 Tbsp. of eggs. Combine spinach, feta cheese, garlic, pepper and remaining beaten eggs.

2. Unroll pizza crust; roll into a 12-in. square. Cut into four 6-in. squares. Top each square with about ⅓ cup spinach mixture. Fold into a triangle and pinch edges to seal. Cut slits in top; brush with reserved egg.

3. In batches if necessary, place triangles in a single layer on greased tray in air-fryer basket. Cook until golden brown, 10-12 minutes. If desired, serve with tzatziki sauce.

1 turnover: 361 cal., 9g fat (4g sat. fat), 104mg chol., 936mg sod., 51g carb. (7g sugars, 4g fiber), 17g pro.

AIR FRYER

ROASTED SALMON WITH SAUTEED BALSAMIC SPINACH

This is my favorite way to eat salmon. The dish is healthy, affordable, fast and delicious.
—Susan Hall, Sparks, MD

TAKES: 30 MIN. • MAKES: 4 SERVINGS

- 3 tsp. olive oil, divided
- 4 salmon fillets (6 oz. each)
- 1½ tsp. reduced-sodium seafood seasoning
- ¼ tsp. pepper
- 1 garlic clove, sliced
- Dash crushed red pepper flakes
- 10 cups fresh baby spinach (about 10 oz.)
- 6 small tomatoes, seeded and cut into ½-in. pieces
- ½ cup balsamic vinegar

1. Preheat air fryer to 450°. Rub 1 tsp. oil over both sides of salmon; sprinkle with seafood seasoning and pepper. In batches if necessary, place salmon on greased tray in air-fryer basket. Cook until fish just begins to flake easily with a fork, 10-12 minutes.

2. Meanwhile, place remaining oil, garlic and pepper flakes in a 6-qt. stockpot; heat over medium-low heat until garlic is softened, 3-4 minutes. Increase heat to medium-high. Add spinach; cook and stir until wilted, 3-4 minutes. Stir in tomatoes; heat through. Divide among 4 serving dishes.

3. In a small saucepan, bring vinegar to a boil. Cook until vinegar is reduced by half, 2-3 minutes. Immediately remove from heat.

4. To serve, place salmon over spinach mixture. Drizzle with balsamic glaze.

1 serving: 348 cal., 19g fat (4g sat. fat), 85mg chol., 286mg sod., 12g carb. (9g sugars, 2g fiber), 31g pro.

ROASTED SALMON WITH
SAUTEED BALSAMIC SPINACH
AIR FRYER

COCONUT SHRIMP WITH APRICOT SAUCE

COCONUT SHRIMP WITH APRICOT SAUCE

Coconut and panko crumbs give this spicy air-fried shrimp its crunch. It's perfect for an appetizer or for your main meal.

—Debi Mitchell, Flower Mound, TX

TAKES: 30 MIN. • MAKES: 2 SERVINGS

AIR FRYER

- ½ lb. uncooked large shrimp
- ½ cup sweetened shredded coconut
- 3 Tbsp. panko bread crumbs
- 2 large egg whites
- ⅛ tsp. salt
- Dash pepper
- Dash Louisiana-style hot sauce
- 3 Tbsp. all-purpose flour

SAUCE

- ⅓ cup apricot preserves
- ½ tsp. cider vinegar
- Dash crushed red pepper flakes

1. Preheat air fryer to 375°. Peel and devein shrimp, leaving tails on.

2. In a shallow bowl, toss coconut with bread crumbs. In another shallow bowl, whisk egg whites, salt, pepper and hot sauce. Place flour in a third shallow bowl.

3. Dip shrimp in flour to coat lightly; shake off excess. Dip in egg white mixture, then in coconut mixture, patting to help coating adhere.

4. Place shrimp in a single layer on greased tray in air-fryer basket. Cook 4 minutes; turn shrimp and continue cooking until coconut is lightly browned and shrimp turn pink, another 4 minutes.

5. Meanwhile, combine sauce ingredients in a small saucepan; cook and stir over medium-low heat until apricot preserves are melted. Serve shrimp immediately with sauce.

6 shrimp with 2 Tbsp. sauce: 423 cal., 10g fat (8g sat. fat), 138mg chol., 440mg sod., 59g carb. (34g sugars, 2g fiber), 25g pro.

CHICKEN PESTO STUFFED PEPPERS

On busy weeknights, I don't want to spend more than 30 minutes preparing dinner, nor do I want to wash a towering pile of dishes. This recipe delivers without having to sacrifice flavor!
—Olivia Cruz, Greenville, SC

TAKES: 25 MIN. • MAKES: 4 SERVINGS

- 4 medium sweet yellow or orange peppers
- 1½ cups shredded rotisserie chicken
- 1½ cups cooked brown rice
- 1 cup prepared pesto
- ½ cup shredded Havarti cheese
- Fresh basil leaves, optional

1. Preheat air fryer to 400°. Cut peppers lengthwise in half; remove stems and seeds. In batches, place peppers in a single layer on tray in air-fryer basket. Cook until the skin starts to blister and peppers are just tender, 10-15 minutes. Reduce air fryer temperature to 350°.

2. Meanwhile, in a large bowl, combine chicken, rice and pesto. When cool enough to handle, fill peppers with chicken mixture. In batches, cook until heated through, about 5 minutes. Sprinkle with cheese; cook until cheese is melted, 3-5 minutes. If desired, sprinkle with basil.

2 stuffed pepper halves: 521 cal., 31g fat (7g sat. fat), 62mg chol., 865mg sod., 33g carb. (7g sugars, 5g fiber), 25g pro.

TEST KITCHEN TIP: Even if bell peppers are pre-washed, it's good practice to give them another cleaning just to be safe. Rinse under cool water, then dry.

CHICKEN PESTO
STUFFED PEPPERS

SWEET & SOUR PINEAPPLE PORK

SWEET & SOUR PINEAPPLE PORK

Here's a great dish to make on a weeknight, and it's special enough for company, too. The recipe starts with pork tenderloin—which is economical and quick to cook—and it tastes delicious.
—Leigh Rys, Herndon, VA

PREP: 25 MIN. • COOK: 15 MIN. • MAKES: 4 SERVINGS

AIR FRYER

- 1 can (8 oz.) unsweetened crushed pineapple, undrained
- 1 cup cider vinegar
- ½ cup sugar
- ½ cup packed dark brown sugar
- ½ cup ketchup
- 2 Tbsp. reduced-sodium soy sauce
- 1 Tbsp. Dijon mustard
- 1 tsp. garlic powder
- 2 pork tenderloins (¾ lb. each), halved
- ¼ tsp. salt
- ¼ tsp. pepper
- Sliced green onions, optional

1. In a large saucepan, combine first 8 ingredients. Bring to a boil; reduce heat. Simmer, uncovered, until thickened, 15-20 minutes, stirring occasionally.

2. Preheat air fryer to 350°. Sprinkle pork with salt and pepper. Place pork on greased tray in air-fryer basket. Cook until pork begins to brown around edges, 7-8 minutes. Turn; pour ¼ cup sauce over pork. Cook until a thermometer inserted into pork reads at least 145°, 10-12 minutes longer. Let pork stand 5 minutes before slicing. Serve with remaining sauce. If desired, top with sliced green onions.

5 oz. cooked pork with ½ cup sauce: 489 cal., 6g fat (2g sat. fat), 95mg chol., 985mg sod., 71g carb. (68g sugars, 1g fiber), 35g pro.

FRIED AVOCADO TACOS

Taco Tuesday just got more exciting! Avocado fans won't be able to get enough of these juicy, flavorful, easy and healthy tacos.
—Julie Peterson, Crofton, MD

PREP: 30 MIN. • COOK: 10 MIN./BATCH • MAKES: 4 SERVINGS

AIR FRYER

- 2 cups shredded fresh kale or coleslaw mix
- ¼ cup minced fresh cilantro
- ¼ cup plain Greek yogurt
- 2 Tbsp. lime juice
- 1 tsp. honey
- ¼ tsp. salt
- ¼ tsp. ground chipotle pepper
- ¼ tsp. pepper

TACOS

- 1 large egg, beaten
- ¼ cup cornmeal
- ½ tsp. salt
- ½ tsp. garlic powder
- ½ tsp. ground chipotle pepper
- 2 medium avocados, peeled and sliced
- Cooking spray
- 8 flour tortillas or corn tortillas (6 in.)
- 1 medium tomato, chopped
- Crumbled queso fresco, optional

1. Combine first 8 ingredients in a bowl. Refrigerate, covered, until serving.

2. Preheat air fryer to 400°. Place egg in a shallow bowl. In another shallow bowl, mix cornmeal, salt, garlic powder and chipotle pepper. Dip avocado slices in egg, then into cornmeal mixture, gently patting to help adhere.

3. In batches, place the avocado slices in a single layer on greased tray in air-fryer basket; spritz with cooking spray. Cook until golden brown, 4 minutes. Turn; spritz with cooking spray. Cook until golden brown, 3-4 minutes longer. Serve avocado slices in tortillas with kale mix, tomato, additional minced cilantro and if desired, queso fresco.

2 tacos: 407 cal., 21g fat (5g sat. fat), 39mg chol., 738mg sod., 48g carb. (4g sugars, 9g fiber), 9g pro.

TEST KITCHEN TIP: Here's a clever hack to try if your avocado is not quite ripe but not hard, either. Cut the avocado in half, remove the pit and wrap each half in microwave-safe plastic wrap. Microwave on high for 2 minutes. Let it cool until easy to handle, then run the wrapped halves under cold water to stop the cooking. Unwrap and use as directed in the recipe.

AIR FRYER

FRIED
AVOCADO TACOS

NACHO DOGS

NACHO DOGS

Adults and kids alike will love these yummy Southwest-inspired hot dogs. This dinner is not only budget-friendly but it's hot, cheesy and delicious, too.

—Joan Hallford, North Richland Hills, TX

PREP: 20 MIN. • COOK: 15 MIN. • MAKES: 6 SERVINGS

- 6 hot dogs
- 3 cheddar cheese sticks, halved lengthwise
- 1¼ cups self-rising flour
- 1 cup plain Greek yogurt
- ¼ cup salsa
- ¼ tsp. chili powder
- 3 Tbsp. chopped seeded jalapeno pepper
- 1 cup crushed nacho-flavored tortilla chips, divided
- Guacamole and sour cream, optional

1. Cut a slit down the length of each hot dog without cutting through; insert a halved cheese stick into the slit. Set aside.

2. Preheat air fryer to 350°. In a large bowl, stir together flour, yogurt, salsa, chili powder, jalapenos and ¼ cup crushed tortilla chips to form a soft dough. Place dough on a lightly floured surface; divide into 6 pieces. Roll dough into 15-in.-long strips; wrap 1 strip around cheese-stuffed hot dog. Repeat with remaining dough and hot dogs. Spray dogs with cooking spray and gently roll in remaining crushed chips. Spray air-fryer basket with cooking spray, and place dogs in basket without touching, leaving room to expand.

3. In batches, cook until dough is slightly browned and cheese starts to melt, 8-10 minutes. If desired, serve with additional salsa, sour cream and guacamole.

1 serving: 216 cal., 9g fat (5g sat. fat), 23mg chol., 513mg sod., 26g carb. (3g sugars, 1g fiber), 9g pro.

ROSEMARY-LEMON CHICKEN THIGHS

These aromatic chicken thighs remind me of something you'd serve at a traditional Sunday dinner. The lemon and herb butter makes the meat flavorful and juicy. If you don't have an air fryer, bake the chicken in the oven at 400° for about 45 minutes.
—Alyssa Lang, North Scituate, RI

PREP: 10 MIN. • COOK: 30 MIN. • MAKES: 4 SERVINGS

AIR FRYER

- ¼ cup butter, softened
- 3 garlic cloves, minced
- 2 tsp. minced fresh rosemary or ½ tsp. dried rosemary, crushed
- 1 tsp. minced fresh thyme or ¼ tsp. dried thyme
- 1 tsp. grated lemon zest
- 1 Tbsp. lemon juice
- 4 bone-in chicken thighs (about 1½ lbs.)
- ⅛ tsp. salt
- ⅛ tsp. pepper

1. Preheat air fryer to 400°. In a small bowl, combine butter, garlic, rosemary, thyme, lemon zest and lemon juice. Spread 1 tsp. butter mixture under skin of each chicken thigh. Spread remaining butter over the skin of each thigh. Sprinkle with salt and pepper.

2. Place chicken, skin side up, on greased tray in air-fryer basket. Cook 20 minutes, turning once. Turn chicken again (skin side up) and cook until a thermometer reads 170°-175°, about 5 minutes.

1 chicken thigh: 329 cal., 26g fat (11g sat. fat), 111mg chol., 234mg sod., 1g carb. (0 sugars, 0 fiber), 23g pro.

WHY YOU'LL LOVE IT...

"Simple, easy to make and very flavorful! I love using my air fryer so I'll definitely make this again!"

—KATE629, TASTEOFHOME.COM

ROSEMARY-LEMON
CHICKEN THIGHS

CHICKEN PARMESAN

CHICKEN PARMESAN

Quick, simple and oh-so-tasty, this air-fried chicken Parmesan is the perfect weeknight dish to have on hand. It's just as crispy as the classic baked version, if not crispier!
—Taste of Home *Test Kitchen*

TAKES: 20 MIN. • MAKES: 4 SERVINGS

- 2 large eggs
- ½ cup seasoned bread crumbs
- ⅓ cup grated Parmesan cheese
- ¼ tsp. pepper
- 4 boneless skinless chicken breast halves (6 oz. each)
- 1 cup pasta sauce
- 1 cup shredded mozzarella cheese
- Chopped fresh basil, optional

1. Preheat air-fryer to 375°. In a shallow bowl, lightly beat eggs. In another shallow bowl, combine bread crumbs and Parmesan cheese and pepper. Dip chicken in egg, then coat with crumb mixture.

2. Place chicken in a single layer on tray in air-fryer basket. Cook until a thermometer reads 165°, 10-12 minutes, turning halfway through. Top chicken with sauce and cheese. Cook until cheese is melted, 3-4 minutes. If desired, sprinkle with basil.

1 chicken breast half: 416 cal., 16g fat (7g sat. fat), 215mg chol., 863mg sod., 18g carb. (6g sugars, 2g fiber), 49g pro.

LEMON FETA CHICKEN

This bright, Greek-inspired chicken has only five ingredients. It's a busy-day lifesaver, and popping it into the air fryer makes it even easier.
—Ann Cain, Morrill, NE

TAKES: 25 MIN. • MAKES: 2 SERVINGS

- 2 boneless skinless chicken breast halves (2 oz. each)
- 1 to 2 Tbsp. lemon juice
- 2 Tbsp. crumbled feta cheese
- ½ tsp. dried oregano
- ¼ tsp. pepper

1. Preheat air fryer to 400°. Place chicken in a lightly greased baking dish that fits into the air fryer. Pour lemon juice over chicken; sprinkle with feta cheese, oregano and pepper.

2. Cook until a thermometer reads 165°, 20-25 minutes.

1 chicken breast half: 142 cal., 4g fat (2g sat. fat), 66mg chol., 122mg sod., 1g carb. (0 sugars, 0 fiber), 24g pro.

AIR FRYER

BACON EGG CUPS

These adorable bacon egg cups are a fresh take on the classic breakfast combo. I originally baked these, but they're amazing in the air fryer—no need to heat up the oven!

—Carol Forcum, Marion, IL

PREP: 20 MIN. • COOK: 15 MIN. • MAKES: 2 SERVINGS

- 4 bacon strips
- 4 large eggs
- ⅓ cup half-and-half cream
- ⅛ tsp. pepper
- ½ cup shredded cheddar cheese
- 2 green onions, chopped

1. In a small skillet, cook bacon over medium heat until cooked but not crisp. Remove to paper towels to drain; keep warm.

2. Preheat air fryer to 350°. In a small bowl, whisk 2 eggs, cream and pepper. Wrap 2 bacon strips around the inside edges of each of two 8-oz. ramekins or custard cups coated with cooking spray.

3. Sprinkle each with half of the cheese and onions. Divide egg mixture between 2 ramekins. Break 1 of the remaining eggs into each ramekin. Sprinkle with remaining cheese and onion. Place ramekins on tray in air-fryer basket; cook until eggs are completely set, 15-20 minutes. Remove from basket; let stand 5 minutes before serving.

1 serving: 397 cal., 29g fat (13g sat. fat), 437mg chol., 640mg sod., 4g carb. (2g sugars, 0 fiber), 26g pro.

BACON EGG CUPS

CHICKEN
THIGHS

CHICKEN THIGHS

This air-fryer chicken thigh recipe creates meat that is crispy on the outside but incredibly juicy on the inside. The paprika and garlic seasoning blend comes through beautifully.
—Taste of Home *Test Kitchen*

TAKES: 20 MIN. • MAKES: 4 SERVINGS

AIR FRYER

- 4 bone-in chicken thighs (about 1½ lbs.)
- 1 Tbsp. olive oil
- ¾ tsp. salt
- ½ tsp. paprika
- ¼ tsp. garlic powder
- ¼ tsp. pepper

Preheat air fryer to 375°. Brush chicken with oil. Combine the remaining ingredients; sprinkle over chicken. Place chicken, skin side up, in a single layer on tray in air-fryer basket. Cook until a thermometer inserted in the chicken reads 170°-175°, 15-17 minutes.

1 chicken thigh: 255 cal., 18g fat (4g sat. fat), 81mg chol., 511mg sod., 0 carb. (0 sugars, 0 fiber), 23g pro.

TEST KITCHEN TIP: After returning home from the grocery store, be sure to place raw chicken in the fridge or freezer right away. It should not be sitting out on the countertop for any length of time. Raw chicken should only be stored in the refrigerator for 2 days before cooking or freezing. Remember to always store chicken on the bottom shelf in the fridge in case juices from the package leak out. Storing on the bottom shelf will avoid contamination to other foods.

CHICKEN TACO POCKETS

We love these easy taco-flavored sandwiches made with crescent dough. They make a quick and easy lunch or supper paired with a bowl of soup or a crisp salad. I also like to cut them into smaller servings and serve them as appetizers at parties.
—Donna Gribbins, Shelbyville, KY

TAKES: 25 MIN. • MAKES: 8 SERVINGS

AIR FRYER

- 2 tubes (8 oz. each) refrigerated crescent rolls
- ½ cup salsa, plus more for serving
- ½ cup sour cream
- 2 Tbsp. taco seasoning
- 1 cup shredded rotisserie chicken
- 1 cup shredded cheddar cheese
- Optional: Shredded lettuce, guacamole and additional sour cream

1. Preheat air fryer to 375°. Unroll 1 tube crescent dough and separate into 2 rectangles; press perforations to seal. Repeat with the second tube. In a bowl, combine salsa, sour cream and taco seasoning. Spoon chicken onto left side of each rectangle; top with salsa mixture. Sprinkle with cheese. Fold dough over filling; pinch edges to seal.

2. In batches if necessary, place pockets on tray in air-fryer basket. Cook until golden brown, 13-15 minutes. Cut in half. Serve with salsa and desired optional toppings.

½ pocket: 393 cal., 24g fat (7g sat. fat), 47mg chol., 896mg sod., 29g carb. (7g sugars, 0 fiber), 16g pro.

CHICKEN TACO POCKETS

MAPLE-
DIJON SALMON

MAPLE-DIJON SALMON

Being landlocked in the Midwest, my kids never gravitated towards fish. This salmon changed their minds! I cook it on the grill in summer, but found that it is just as tasty and more convenient in the air fryer, especially on busy days.

—Jill Fisher, Portland, IN

TAKES: 25 MIN. • MAKES: 4 SERVINGS

AIR FRYER

- 3 Tbsp. butter
- 3 Tbsp. maple syrup
- 1 Tbsp. Dijon mustard
- 1 medium lemon (juiced)
- 1 garlic clove, minced
- 1 Tbsp. olive oil
- ¼ tsp. salt
- ¼ tsp. pepper
- 4 salmon fillets (4 oz. each)

Preheat air fryer to 400°. Meanwhile, in a small saucepan melt butter over medium-high heat. Add maple syrup, mustard, lemon juice and minced garlic. Reduce heat and simmer until mixture thickens slightly, 2-3 minutes. Remove from heat; set aside. Drizzle olive oil over salmon and sprinkle with salt and pepper. Place fish in a single layer in air-fryer basket. Cook until fish is lightly browned and just beginning to flake easily with a fork, 5-7 minutes. Drizzle with sauce right before serving.

1 fillet: 329 cal., 23g fat (8g sat. fat), 80mg chol., 365mg sod., 11g carb. (9g sugars, 0 fiber), 19g pro.

TEST KITCHEN TIP: An easy way to test when salmon has finished cooking is to use the flake test: Press down on the top of the fillet with a fork. If the salmon flakes or separates along the lines of its flesh, it's finished cooking. Its flesh should look opaque.

SPICY GINGER BEEF SKEWERS

We love the flavors of these zippy kabobs. I usually cook them outside on the grill, but if it's cold or rainy, I take advantage of my air fryer.

—Jasey McBurnett, Rock Springs, WY

PREP: 20 MIN. + MARINATING • COOK: 5 MIN. • MAKES: 6 SERVINGS

AIR FRYER

- 1 beef flank steak (1½ lbs.)
- 1 cup rice vinegar
- 1 cup soy sauce
- ¼ cup packed brown sugar
- 2 Tbsp. minced fresh gingerroot
- 6 garlic cloves, minced
- 3 tsp. sesame oil
- 2 tsp. Sriracha chili sauce or 1 tsp. hot pepper sauce
- ½ tsp. cornstarch
- Optional: Sesame seeds and thinly sliced green onions

1. Cut beef into ¼-in.-thick strips. In a large bowl, whisk the next 7 ingredients until blended. Pour 1 cup marinade into a shallow dish. Add beef; turn to coat. Refrigerate, covered, 2-8 hours. Cover and refrigerate remaining marinade.

2. Preheat air fryer to 400°. Drain beef, discarding marinade in dish. Thread the beef onto 12 metal or soaked wooden skewers that fit into air fryer. In batches if necessary, arrange skewers in a single layer on greased tray in air-fryer basket. Cook until meat reaches desired doneness (for medium-rare, a thermometer should read 135°; medium, 140°; medium-well, 145°), 4-5 minutes, turning occasionally and basting frequently using ½ cup of reserved marinade.

3. Meanwhile, to make glaze, bring remaining marinade (about ¾ cup) to a boil; whisk in ½ tsp. cornstarch. Cook, whisking constantly until thickened, 1-2 minutes. Brush skewers with glaze just before serving. If desired, top with sesame seeds and sliced green onions.

2 kabobs: 264 cal., 10g fat (4g sat. fat), 54mg chol., 1480mg sod., 18g carb. (15g sugars, 0 fiber), 24g pro.

SPICY GINGER BEEF SKEWERS

DESSERTS

CARROT COFFEE CAKE, PAGE 204

PECAN STRAWBERRY
RHUBARB COBBLER

PECAN STRAWBERRY RHUBARB COBBLER

Chock-full of berries and rhubarb, this pretty cobbler is the perfect finale for a dinner for two. Both the pecans in the topping and the delicious dessert sauce make it extra special.

—Lily Julow, Lawrenceville, GA

PREP: 20 MIN. + STANDING • COOK: 25 MIN. • MAKES: 2 SERVINGS

AIR FRYER

- 1 cup sliced fresh or frozen rhubarb
- 1 cup sliced fresh strawberries
- ¼ cup sugar
- 1 Tbsp. quick-cooking tapioca
- 1 tsp. lemon juice
- Dash salt

TOPPING

- ⅓ cup all-purpose flour
- ¼ cup chopped pecans
- 3 Tbsp. sugar
- ⅛ tsp. baking powder
- Dash salt
- 2 Tbsp. cold butter
- 1 large egg, room temperature

SAUCE

- ½ cup vanilla ice cream
- 2¼ tsp. Marsala wine

1. Preheat air fryer to 375°. Combine the first 6 ingredients; divide between 2 greased 8-oz. ramekins or custard cups. Let stand for 15 minutes.

2. In a small bowl, combine flour, pecans, sugar, baking powder and salt; cut in butter until mixture resembles coarse crumbs. Stir in egg. Drop by spoonfuls over fruit mixture; spread evenly.

3. Place ramekins on tray in air-fryer basket. Cook until filling is bubbly and a toothpick inserted in topping comes out clean, 25-30 minutes.

4. In a microwave-safe bowl, combine ice cream and wine. Cook, uncovered, at 50% power for 1-2 minutes or until heated through; stir until blended. Serve with warm cobbler.

1 cobbler: 615 cal., 28g fat (11g sat. fat), 138mg chol., 335mg sod., 85g carb. (57g sugars, 5g fiber), 9g pro.

CARROT COFFEE CAKE

One of the greatest things about the air fryer is that it's conducive to making small, quick desserts and breakfast treats. The little cake bakes in about 30 minutes and is perfect for enjoying with your morning coffee.

—Leigh Rys, Herndon, VA

PREP: 15 MIN. • BAKE: 35 MIN. • MAKES: 6 SERVINGS

- 1 large egg, lightly beaten, room temperature
- ½ cup buttermilk
- ⅓ cup sugar plus 2 Tbsp. sugar, divided
- 3 Tbsp. canola oil
- 2 Tbsp. dark brown sugar
- 1 tsp. grated orange zest
- 1 tsp. vanilla extract
- ⅔ cup all-purpose flour
- ⅓ cup white whole wheat flour
- 1 tsp. baking powder
- 2 tsp. pumpkin pie spice, divided
- ¼ tsp. baking soda
- ¼ tsp. salt
- 1 cup shredded carrots
- ¼ cup dried cranberries
- ⅓ cup chopped walnuts, toasted

1. Preheat air fryer to 350°. Grease and flour a 6-in. round baking pan. In a large bowl, whisk egg, buttermilk, ⅓ cup sugar, oil, brown sugar, orange zest and vanilla. In another bowl, whisk flours, baking powder, 1 tsp. pumpkin pie spice, baking soda and salt. Gradually beat into egg mixture. Fold in carrots and dried cranberries. Pour into prepared pan.

2. In a small bowl, combine walnuts, remaining 2 Tbsp. sugar and remaining 1 tsp. pumpkin spice. Sprinkle evenly over batter. Gently place pan in basket of a large air fryer.

3. Cook until a toothpick inserted in center comes out clean, 35-40 minutes. Cover tightly with foil if top gets too dark. Cool in pan on a wire rack for 10 minutes before removing from pan. Serve warm.

1 piece: 316 cal., 13g fat (1g sat. fat), 32mg chol., 297mg sod., 46g carb. (27g sugars, 3g fiber), 6g pro.

CARROT COFFEE CAKE

MINI NUTELLA
DOUGHNUT HOLES

MINI NUTELLA DOUGHNUT HOLES

You can make these doughnuts in advance and refrigerate them before cooking. Just be sure to bring the dough to room temperature before putting them in the air fryer.

—Renee Murphy, Smithtown, NY

PREP: 30 MIN. • COOK: 5 MIN./BATCH • MAKES: 32 DOUGHNUTS

AIR FRYER

- 1 large egg
- 1 Tbsp. water
- 1 tube (16.3 oz.) large refrigerated flaky biscuits (8 count)
- ⅔ cup Nutella
- Confectioners' sugar

1. Preheat air fryer to 300°. Whisk egg with water. On a lightly floured surface, roll each biscuit into a 6-in. circle; cut each into 4 wedges. Brush lightly with egg mixture; top each wedge with 1 tsp. Nutella. Bring up corners over filling; pinch edges firmly to seal.

2. In batches, arrange the biscuits in a single layer on ungreased tray in the air-fryer basket. Cook until golden brown, 8-10 minutes, turning once. Dust with confectioners' sugar; serve warm.

1 doughnut: 94 cal., 6g fat (1g sat. fat), 6mg chol., 119mg sod., 10g carb. (4g sugars, 0 fiber), 1g pro.

WHY YOU'LL LOVE IT...

"I am so addicted to these! The recipe makes so many, and I could have eaten them all—delicious!"

—BONITO15, TASTEOFHOME.COM

AIR FRYER

MOCHA PUDDING CAKES

These mouthwatering mini cakes make the perfect treat for two. My mom used to make these when I was a little girl. Now I whip them up and pop them into my air fryer for a speedy dessert.
—Debora Simmons, Eglon, WV

TAKES: 30 MIN. • MAKES: 2 SERVINGS

- ¼ cup all-purpose flour
- 3 Tbsp. sugar
- 1½ tsp. baking cocoa
- ½ tsp. baking powder
- ⅛ tsp. salt
- 3 Tbsp. 2% milk
- 1½ tsp. butter, melted
- ¼ tsp. vanilla extract

TOPPING

- 2 Tbsp. brown sugar
- 1½ tsp. baking cocoa
- 3 Tbsp. hot brewed coffee
- 1 Tbsp. hot water
- Whipped topping, optional

1. Preheat air fryer to 350°. In a small bowl, combine flour, sugar, cocoa, baking powder and salt. Stir in milk, butter and vanilla until smooth. Spoon into 2 lightly greased 4-oz. ramekins. Combine brown sugar and cocoa; sprinkle over batter. Combine coffee and water; pour over topping.

2. Place ramekins on tray in air-fryer basket. Cook until a knife inserted in the center comes out clean,15-20 minutes. Serve warm or at room temperature, with whipped topping if desired.

1 pudding cake: 229 cal., 4g fat (2g sat. fat), 9mg chol., 306mg sod., 47g carb. (33g sugars, 1g fiber), 3g pro.

WHY YOU'LL LOVE IT...

"This is one of my favorite recipes! Everyone I've made it for asks for the recipe."

—MARISSARN, TASTEOFHOME.COM

MOCHA
PUDDING CAKES

APPLE FRITTERS WITH BROWN BUTTER GLAZE

APPLE FRITTERS WITH BROWN BUTTER GLAZE

An air fryer makes these easy breakfast bites healthier than classic deep-fried fritters, yet they are still as delicious. They're ready in under 30 minutes—including a scrumptious brown butter glaze—for a quick and easy dessert!

—Alyssa Lang, North Scituate, RI

PREP: 10 MIN. • COOK: 8 MIN./BATCH • MAKES: 15 SERVINGS

AIR FRYER

- Cooking spray
- 1½ cups all-purpose flour
- ¼ cup sugar
- 2 tsp. baking powder
- 1½ tsp. ground cinnamon
- ½ tsp. salt
- ⅔ cup 2% milk
- 2 large eggs, room temperature
- 1 Tbsp. lemon juice
- 1½ tsp. vanilla extract, divided
- 2 medium Honeycrisp apples, peeled and chopped
- ¼ cup butter
- 1 cup confectioners' sugar
- 1 Tbsp. 2% milk

1. Line air-fryer basket with parchment (cut to fit); spritz with cooking spray.

2. Preheat air fryer to 410°. In a large bowl, combine the flour, sugar, baking powder, cinnamon and salt. Add milk, eggs, lemon juice and 1 tsp. vanilla extract; stir just until moistened. Fold in apples.

3. In batches, drop dough by ¼ cupfuls 2 in. apart onto air-fryer basket. Spritz with cooking spray. Cook until golden brown, 5-6 minutes. Turn fritters; continue to air-fry until golden brown, 1-2 minutes.

4. Melt butter in small saucepan over medium-high heat. Carefully cook until butter starts to brown and foam, 5 minutes. Remove from heat; cool slightly. Add confectioners' sugar, 1 Tbsp. milk and remaining ½ tsp. vanilla extract to browned butter; whisk until smooth. Drizzle over fritters before serving.

1 fritter: 145 cal., 4g fat (2g sat. fat), 34mg chol., 183mg sod., 24g carb. (14g sugars, 1g fiber), 3g pro.
Diabetic exchanges: 1 fat.

PEPPERMINT LAVA CAKES

Warm chocolate pudding oozes out of the centers of these tender chocolate cakes. They're a showstopper on a plate. Serve with whipped cream or ice cream.

—Carolyn Crotser, Colorado Springs, CO

TAKES: 30 MIN. • MAKES: 4 SERVINGS

AIR FRYER

- ⅔ cup semisweet chocolate chips
- ½ cup butter, cubed
- 1 cup confectioners' sugar
- 2 large eggs, room temperature
- 2 large egg yolks, room temperature
- 1 tsp. peppermint extract
- 6 Tbsp. all-purpose flour
- 2 Tbsp. finely crushed peppermint candies, optional

1. Preheat air fryer to 375°. In a microwave-safe bowl, melt chocolate chips and butter for 30 seconds; stir until smooth. Whisk in confectioners' sugar, eggs, egg yolks and extract until blended. Fold in flour.

2. Generously grease and flour four 4-oz. ramekins; pour the batter into ramekins. Do not overfill. Place ramekins on tray in air-fryer basket; cook until a thermometer reads 160° and edges of cakes are set, 10-12 minutes. Do not overcook.

3. Remove from basket; let stand 5 minutes. Carefully run a knife around sides of ramekins several times to loosen cake; invert onto dessert plates. Sprinkle with crushed candies. Serve immediately.

1 serving: 563 cal., 36g fat (21g sat. fat), 246mg chol., 226mg sod., 57g carb. (45g sugars, 2g fiber), 7g pro.

WHY YOU'LL LOVE IT...

"These were absolutely delicious. I didn't have peppermint so I substituted a teaspoon of vanilla. The gooey lava center was out-of-this-world good. A perfect dinner party dessert, it comes together and cooks quickly."

—OLIVEDOG, TASTEOFHOME.COM

PEPPERMINT LAVA CAKES

HONEYED PEARS
IN PUFF PASTRY

HONEYED PEARS IN PUFF PASTRY

A honey of a salute to late-summer pear season, this cozy dessert is both elegant and decadent. Wrapped in puff pastry, the pears resemble little beehives.
—Heather Baird, Knoxville, TN

PREP: 25 MIN. • COOK: 15 MIN. • MAKES: 4 SERVINGS

AIR FRYER

- 4 small pears
- 4 cups water
- 2 cups sugar
- 1 cup honey
- 1 small lemon, halved
- 3 cinnamon sticks (3 in.)
- 6 to 8 whole cloves
- 1 vanilla bean
- 1 sheet frozen puff pastry, thawed
- 1 large egg, lightly beaten

1. Core pears from bottom, leaving stems intact. Peel pears; cut ¼ in. from the bottom of each to level if necessary.

2. In a large saucepan, combine water, sugar, honey, lemon halves, cinnamon and cloves. Split vanilla bean and scrape seeds; add bean and seeds to sugar mixture. Bring to a boil. Reduce the heat; place the pears on their sides in saucepan and poach, uncovered, until almost tender, basting occasionally with poaching liquid, 16-20 minutes.

3. Remove the pears with a slotted spoon; cool slightly. Strain and reserve 1½ cups poaching liquid; set aside.

4. Preheat air fryer to 325°. Unfold puff pastry on a lightly floured surface. Cut into ½-in.-wide strips. Brush lightly with beaten egg. Starting at the bottom of a pear, wrap a pastry strip around pear, adding additional strips until pear is completely wrapped in pastry. Repeat with remaining pears and puff pastry.

5. Place pears in a single layer on greased tray in air-fryer basket. Cook until golden brown, 12-15 minutes.

6. Meanwhile, bring reserved poaching liquid to a boil; cook until liquid is thick and syrupy, about 10 minutes. Place pears on dessert plates and drizzle with syrup. Serve warm.

1 pear with 3 Tbsp. syrup: 536 cal., 18g fat (4g sat. fat), 47mg chol., 223mg sod., 92g carb. (50g sugars, 9g fiber), 7g pro.

CHOCOLATE CHIP OATMEAL COOKIES

I am crazy about chocolate chips, and these chewy cookies have enough to satisfy me. My husband and kids love them, too. This big batch is perfect, even for our small family.

—Diane Neth, Menno, SD

PREP: 20 MIN. • COOK: 10 MIN./BATCH • MAKES: 6 DOZEN

AIR FRYER

- 1 cup butter, softened
- ¾ cup sugar
- ¾ cup packed brown sugar
- 2 large eggs, room temperature
- 1 tsp. vanilla extract
- 3 cups quick-cooking oats
- 1½ cups all-purpose flour
- 1 pkg. (3.4 oz.) instant vanilla pudding mix
- 1 tsp. baking soda
- 1 tsp. salt
- 2 cups semisweet chocolate chips
- 1 cup chopped nuts

1. Preheat air fryer to 325°. In a large bowl, cream butter and sugars until light and fluffy, 5-7 minutes. Beat in eggs and vanilla. In another bowl, whisk the oats, flour, dry pudding mix, baking soda and salt; gradually beat into creamed mixture. Stir in chocolate chips and nuts.

2. Drop the dough by tablespoonfuls onto baking sheets; flatten slightly. In batches, place 1 in. apart on greased tray in air-fryer basket. Cook until lightly browned, 8-10 minutes. Remove to wire racks to cool.

1 cookie: 102 cal., 5g fat (3g sat. fat), 12mg chol., 82mg sod., 13g carb. (8g sugars, 1g fiber), 2g pro.

WHY YOU'LL LOVE IT...

"These cookies were amazing! Chewy and delicious. Only took 6-8 minutes in our air fryer. Will absolutely make these again."

—BECKYSPACKE, TASTEOFHOME.COM

CHOCOLATE CHIP
OATMEAL COOKIES

LIP-SMACKING PEACH & WHISKEY WINGS, PAGE 237

SLOW COOKER

To our dear hardworking slow cookers, thank you for the many warm welcome-homes! Thanks for freeing up holiday oven space, for making us the most put-together party hosts on the block, and for being the all-around potluck star that you are. We love you!

SLOW COOKER 101

Slow cookers are truly kitchen superstars. This dependable appliance makes cooking a hot and hearty meal for the family uncomplicated, plus they are easy to care for and can last for years. Follow these easy tips for slow-cooking success every time.

- Begin by reading your recipe. You want to make sure you have all of the ingredients on hand and enough time for your food to properly cook in the slow cooker before mealtime.

- Plan ahead so you can easily prep, toss, plug in and go. In most cases, you can prepare and load ingredients into the slow-cooker insert beforehand and store it in the refrigerator overnight. But be aware that your slow cooker's insert can crack if exposed to rapid temperature changes. Let the insert sit out just long enough to reach room temperature (20-30 minutes) before placing in the slow cooker.

- Use thawed ingredients. Although throwing frozen chicken breasts into the slow cooker may seem easy, it's not a smart shortcut. Thawing foods in a slow cooker can create the ideal environment for bacteria to grow, so thaw frozen meat and veggies ahead of time. The only exception is if you're using a prepackaged slow-cooker meal kit that's intended to be pulled from the freezer and tossed in the slow cooker. For optimal results, always follow the instructions as written.

- Choose the right cut of meat. While you can cook just about any meat in a slow-cooker, we recommend avoiding dry meat by choosing cuts that are tougher or have a higher fat content, as these cuts hold up better to long-term cooking. This means chicken thighs over chicken breasts, pork shoulder over tenderloin and beef chuck roast over strip steak. Trim excess fat from the outside, but look for good marbling on the inside. It will break down during cooking and make the meat tender.

- Take the time to brown. Give yourself a few extra minutes to brown the meat in a pan before placing it in the slow cooker. Doing so adds rich color and flavor to the dish.

- Make use of smart layering. Layer dense foods that take longer to cook, like potatoes, in the bottom of the slow cooker. This way they are closer to the heat than items layered on top. For best results, always follow your recipe's instructions for layering.

- Don't overfill or under-fill. Fill the slow cooker between half and two-thirds full. Less than half full, and the food may burn. More than two-thirds full, and the food may not cook completely.

HOW TO CLEAN YOUR SLOW COOKER

ALLOW the stoneware insert to cool before rinsing it. Wash it in the dishwasher or in the sink with warm, soapy water.

DO not use harsh or abrasive cleansers.

USE a damp sponge to clean the metal base. Do not soak the base in water.

TO remove white mineral stains from the insert, fill the cooker with hot water mixed with 1 cup of white vinegar and heat on high for 2 hours. Empty the insert, let it cool, and wash as usual.

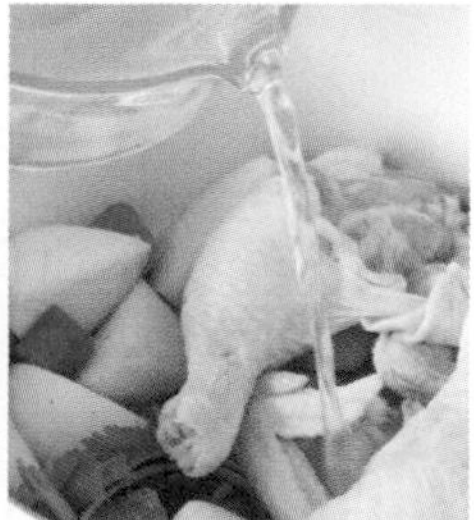

SLOW COOKER

- You should always have a bit of liquid at the base of your slow cooker recipe. This keeps the ingredients from getting too hot, sticking to the bottom of the dish and potentially burning. Great liquids to add are broth, water and even barbecue sauce.

- Go easy when adding alcohol. Alcohol won't evaporate from the slow cooker, so use sparingly. If you brown the meat first, use wine to deglaze the pan, then pour the liquid into the slow cooker. This bit of cooking on the stovetop will burn off the alcohol while preserving all the savory flavor.

- Make sure the lid fits. Be sure the lid is secure, not tilted or askew. Steam held in during cooking creates a seal.

- Don't peek! No matter how tempted you are to look inside, keep that lid on. Each time you lift the lid of your slow cooker, hot steam escapes and you add about 15-30 minutes of cooking time. Most slow cookers come with glass lids to satisfy curious cooks. Open the lid only when the recipe calls for it.

- Don't let your slow cooker (and your food, for that matter) get cold. Most slow cookers have an automatic shut off feature after 24 hours. If you won't be home when the cooking time is up, be sure the cooker will switch itself over to warm. Temperatures between 40° and 140° allow bacteria to thrive.

- Avoid temperature shocks. If your slow cooker has a ceramic insert, put a dish towel or a few hot pads on a cold work surface before placing the hot insert on it. Along those same lines, do not preheat your cooker the way you would preheat an oven. A cold insert should always be put into a cold base.

- Want your food ready sooner? Halve the time by doubling the temperature setting. On most models, low is 170° and high is 280°. For many recipes, cranking up the heat will cut down the cook time. Cooking 1 hour on high is roughly equal to 2 hours on low, so adjust the recipe to suit your schedule.

- If you live at a high altitude, you'll need to adjust the cooking time, as it takes food longer to slow-cook at a high altitude. Add about 30 minutes for each hour of cooking the recipe calls for; legumes will take about twice as long.

- Keep it fresh. Only put foods in the slow cooker that you are cooking for the first time. Don't use your slow cooker to reheat food. Instead, use the microwave, oven or stovetop.

- Some recipes may benefit from a foil sling or collar. A sling helps you lift foods out of the crock without much mess. It also prevents rich, saucy dishes from scorching near the slow cooker's heating element. To make a sling, fold two 18-in.-long pieces of heavy-duty foil into strips about 4 in. wide (see the photos below). Place the strips on the bottom and up the sides of the slow cooker; coat with cooking spray.

HOW TO CONVERT RECIPES FOR THE SLOW COOKER

Almost any recipe that bakes in the oven or simmers on the stovetop can be converted for the slow cooker. Here are some guidelines.

- Select recipes that simmer for at least 45 minutes. Good candidates are soups, stews, pot roasts, chili and other one-dish meals.

- Look for a slow-cooker recipe that's similar to the one you want to convert. Note the quantity and size of the meat and vegetables, heat setting and cooking time.

- A slow cooker doesn't allow for evaporation, so if a recipe calls for liquid, you'll need to use less. If a recipe calls for 6 to 8 cups of water, start with 5 cups. But if the recipe doesn't call for any liquid, add about ½ cup of water, broth or juice—all slow cooker recipes should include some liquid.

COOK TIMES

CONVENTIONAL OVEN	SLOW COOKER
15 to 30 minutes	**Low:** 4 to 6 hours **High:** 1½ to 2 hours
35 to 45 minutes	**Low:** 6 to 8 hours **High:** 3 to 4 hours
50 minutes or more	**Low:** 8 to 10 hours **High:** 4 to 6 hours

SNACKS

SIMMERED SMOKED LINKS, PAGE 226

BUFFALO CHICKEN EGG ROLLS

BUFFALO CHICKEN EGG ROLLS

These crunchy delights get their start in the slow cooker. Tuck the chicken mixture into egg roll wrappers and bake, or use smaller wonton wrappers for a bite-sized version.

—Tara Odegaard, Omaha, NE

PREP: 35 MIN. • COOK: 3 HOURS • MAKES: 16 EGG ROLLS

- 1½ lbs. boneless skinless chicken breasts
- 2 Tbsp. ranch salad dressing mix
- ½ cup Buffalo wing sauce
- 2 Tbsp. butter
- 16 egg roll wrappers
- ⅓ cup crumbled feta cheese
- ⅓ cup shredded part-skim mozzarella cheese
- Ranch salad dressing, optional

1. In a 3-qt. slow cooker, combine chicken, dressing mix and wing sauce. Cook, covered, on low until chicken is tender, 3-4 hours.

2. Preheat oven to 425°. Shred chicken with 2 forks; stir in butter.

3. With a corner of an egg roll wrapper facing you, place 3 Tbsp. chicken mixture just below the center of the wrapper; top with 1 tsp. each feta and mozzarella cheeses. (Cover remaining wrappers with a damp paper towel until ready to use.) Fold the bottom corner over filling; moisten remaining wrapper edges with water. Fold side corners toward center over filling; roll up tightly, pressing at the tip to seal. Place on a parchment-lined baking sheet, seam side down. Repeat, adding additional baking sheets as needed.

4. Bake until golden brown, 15-20 minutes. Let stand 5 minutes before serving. Serve warm, with ranch dressing for dipping if desired.

1 egg roll: 174 cal., 4g fat (2g sat. fat), 33mg chol., 716mg sod., 21g carb. (0 sugars, 1g fiber), 13g pro.

TEST KITCHEN TIP: We brushed some of the egg rolls with oil before baking. Like the plain version, they turned out lightly browned and crisp and had a little extra crunch, similar to deep-fried egg rolls.

CHEESY BRUSCHETTA SPREAD

Every bite of this cheesy dip delivers tons of flavor. I have been asked over and over again for the recipe. It's so easy to make, and it's a great appetizer for any time of year.
—Maggie McDermott, Central Square, NY

PREP: 15 MIN. • COOK: 1½ HOURS • MAKES: ABOUT 4 CUPS

- 1 pkg. (8 oz.) cream cheese, softened
- ½ cup prepared pesto
- ¼ tsp. salt
- ⅛ tsp. pepper
- 2 cups grape tomatoes
- 1 carton (8 oz.) fresh mozzarella cheese pearls, drained
- Minced fresh basil, optional
- French bread slices (½ in. thick), toasted

In a small bowl, mix cream cheese, pesto, salt and pepper until combined. Transfer to a greased 3-qt. slow cooker. Top with tomatoes and mozzarella cheese. Cook, covered, on low until heated though and cheese begins to melt, 1½-2 hours. If desired, sprinkle with basil. Serve with toasted bread.

2 Tbsp.: 61 cal., 5g fat (3g sat. fat), 13mg chol., 96mg sod., 1g carb. (1g sugars, 0 fiber), 2g pro.

SIMMERED SMOKED LINKS

SEE PHOTO ON PAGE 223

No one can resist the sweet and spicy glaze on these bite-sized sausages. They're effortless to prepare, and they make the perfect party nibbler. Serve them on frilled toothpicks to make them extra fancy.
—Maxine Cenker, Weirton, WV

PREP: 5 MIN. • COOK: 4 HOURS • MAKES: ABOUT 6½ DOZEN

- 2 pkg. (16 oz. each) miniature smoked sausage links
- 1 cup packed brown sugar
- ½ cup ketchup
- ¼ cup prepared horseradish

Place sausages in a 3-qt. slow cooker. Combine the brown sugar, ketchup and horseradish; pour over sausages. Cover and cook on low for 4 hours.

1 sausage: 46 cal., 3g fat (1g sat. fat), 7mg chol., 136mg sod., 3g carb. (3g sugars, 0 fiber), 1g pro.

CHEESY BRUSCHETTA SPREAD

CHEESEBURGER DIP

CHEESEBURGER DIP

This fun dip recipe uses ingredients I always have in the fridge, so it's easy to throw together on short notice.

—Cindi DeClue, Anchorage, AK

PREP: 25 MIN. • COOK: 1¾ HOURS • MAKES: 16 SERVINGS

- 1 lb. lean ground beef (90% lean)
- 1 medium onion, chopped
- 1 pkg. (8 oz.) cream cheese, cubed
- 2 cups shredded cheddar cheese, divided
- 1 Tbsp. Worcestershire sauce
- 2 tsp. prepared mustard
- ¼ tsp. salt
- ⅛ tsp. pepper
- 1 medium tomato, chopped
- ¼ cup chopped dill pickles
- Tortilla chips or crackers

1. In a large skillet, cook beef and onion over medium-high heat until beef is no longer pink and the onion is tender, 6-8 minutes, breaking up beef; drain. Transfer to a greased 1½- or 3-qt. slow cooker. Stir in the cream cheese, 1½ cups cheddar cheese, Worcestershire, mustard, salt and pepper. Sprinkle with remaining cheese.

2. Cook dip, covered, on low 1¾-2¼ hours or until mixture is heated through and cheese is melted. Top with chopped tomato and pickles. Serve with tortilla chips or crackers.

¼ cup: 157 cal., 12g fat (6g sat. fat), 46mg chol., 225mg sod., 2g carb. (1g sugars, 0 fiber), 10g pro.

TEST KITCHEN TIP: Keep an eye on the dip toward the end of cooking. If it goes too long, the edges will get dark.

SLOW COOKER

BACK PORCH MEATBALLS

The idea for this recipe came to me while sitting on my back porch. The combination of meats and ingredients in the sauce produces meatballs unlike others I've had.
—Justin Boudreaux, Walker, LA

PREP: 30 MIN. • COOK: 3 HOURS • MAKES: 6 DOZEN

- 2 large eggs, lightly beaten
- 2 cups seasoned bread crumbs
- 2 cups salsa
- ½ cup grated onion
- ⅔ lb. ground turkey
- ⅔ lb. ground pork
- ⅔ lb. ground beef

SLOW COOKER

SAUCE

- 3 cups tomato sauce
- 1 medium onion, grated
- 1 cup beef stock
- 1 cup mixed fruit jelly
- 1 cup molasses
- ½ cup packed brown sugar
- ½ cup canola oil
- ½ cup red wine vinegar
- ⅓ cup prepared mustard
- ⅓ cup Worcestershire sauce
- 1 tsp. salt

1. Preheat oven to 400°. In a large bowl, combine egg, bread crumbs, salsa and onion. Add turkey, pork and beef; mix lightly but thoroughly. Shape into 1½-in. balls. Place the meatballs on greased racks in two 15x10x1-in. baking pans. Bake until meat is browned, 18-22 minutes.

2. In a 6-qt. slow cooker, combine sauce ingredients. Add meatballs; gently stir to coat. Cook, covered, on low until meatballs are cooked through, 3-4 hours.

Freeze option: Freeze cooled meatball mixture in freezer containers. To use, partially thaw in the refrigerator overnight. Microwave, covered, on high in a microwave-safe dish until heated through, gently stirring and adding a little water if necessary.

1 meatball: 87 cal., 3g fat (1g sat. fat), 13mg chol., 195mg sod., 11g carb. (8g sugars, 0 fiber), 3g pro.

BACK PORCH MEATBALLS

CHICKEN CORDON BLEU SLIDERS

CHICKEN CORDON BLEU SLIDERS

Sandwiches are my favorite food, and I'm always looking for new ideas. I like sloppy joes and wondered whether I could do a fun riff on that with chicken. This experiment definitely got my family's approval!

—Carolyn Eskew, Dayton, OH

PREP: 20 MIN. • COOK: 2½ HOURS + STANDING • MAKES: 2 DOZEN

- 1½ lbs. boneless skinless chicken breasts
- 1 garlic clove, minced
- ¼ tsp. salt
- ¼ tsp. pepper
- 1 pkg. (8 oz.) cream cheese, cubed
- 2 cups shredded Swiss cheese
- 1¼ cups finely chopped fully cooked ham
- 2 pkg. (12 oz. each) Hawaiian sweet rolls, split
- Chopped green onions

1. Place chicken in a greased 3-qt. slow cooker; sprinkle with garlic, salt and pepper. Top with cream cheese. Cook, covered, on low, 2½-3 hours or until a thermometer inserted in chicken reads 165°. Remove the chicken; shred with 2 forks. Return to slow cooker.

2. Stir in Swiss cheese and ham. Cover and let stand 15 minutes or until cheese is melted. Stir before serving on rolls. Sprinkle with green onion.

1 slider: 209 cal., 10g fat (5g sat. fat), 53mg chol., 254mg sod., 17g carb. (6g sugars, 1g fiber), 14g pro.

TEST KITCHEN TIP: Suit your tastes by applying an easy variation or two to this recipe. You can use cubed pancetta or crumbled bacon in place of the ham. Shredded provolone works well in place of the Swiss.

CHEDDAR BACON BEER DIP

My tangy, smoky dip won the top prize in our office party recipe contest. Other beers can work, but you should steer clear of dark varieties.

—Ashley Lecker, Green Bay, WI

PREP: 15 MIN. • COOK: 3 HOURS • MAKES: 4½ CUPS

- 18 oz. cream cheese, softened
- ¼ cup sour cream
- 1½ Tbsp. Dijon mustard
- 1 tsp. garlic powder
- 1 cup amber beer or nonalcoholic beer
- 2 cups shredded cheddar cheese
- 1 lb. bacon strips, cooked and crumbled, divided
- ¼ cup heavy whipping cream
- 1 green onion, thinly sliced
- Soft pretzel bites

SLOW COOKER

1. In a greased 3-qt. slow cooker, combine the cream cheese, sour cream, mustard and garlic powder until smooth. Stir in the beer, cheese and all but 2 Tbsp. bacon. Cook, covered, on low, stirring occasionally, until heated through, 3-4 hours.

2. In the last 30 minutes, stir in heavy cream. Top with onion and remaining bacon. Serve with soft pretzel bites.

¼ cup: 213 cal., 19g fat (10g sat. fat), 60mg chol., 378mg sod., 2g carb. (1g sugars, 0 fiber), 8g pro.

TEST KITCHEN TIP: Your favorite ale will also work in this recipe. The Test Kitchen loved the flavor of New Belgium Fat Tire.

CHEDDAR
BACON BEER DIP

LIP-SMACKING PEACH & WHISKEY WINGS

LIP-SMACKING PEACH & WHISKEY WINGS

These sweet, spicy, sticky chicken wings are lip-smacking good! You can use fresh peaches in place of canned if you like. Just add a few tablespoons of brown sugar.

—Sue Falk, Sterling Heights, MI

PREP: 20 MIN. • COOK: 4¼ HOURS • MAKES: 2 DOZEN PIECES

- 3 lbs. chicken wings (about 1 dozen)
- 1 tsp. salt
- ½ tsp. pepper
- 1 can (29 oz.) sliced peaches in extra-light syrup, undrained
- ½ cup whiskey
- ¼ cup honey
- 1 Tbsp. lime juice
- 1 Tbsp. Louisiana-style hot sauce
- 3 garlic cloves, minced
- 4 tsp. cornstarch
- 2 Tbsp. cold water
- Minced chives, optional

1. Pat chicken wings dry. Using a sharp knife, cut through 2 wing joints; discard wing tips. Season wings with salt and pepper. Place in a 3- or 4-qt. slow cooker.

2. Pulse peaches with syrup in a food processor until pureed. Add the next 5 ingredients; pulse to combine. Pour over wings; toss to coat. Cook, covered, on low until chicken is tender, 4-6 hours.

3. Combine the cornstarch and water until smooth; stir into slow cooker. Cook, covered, on high until sauce is thickened, about 15 minutes.

4. Preheat broiler. Remove wings to a 15x10x1-in. pan; arrange in a single layer. Broil wings 3-4 in. from heat until lightly browned, 2-3 minutes. Brush with sauce before serving. Serve with remaining sauce and, if desired, chives.

1 piece: 93 cal., 4g fat (1g sat. fat), 18mg chol., 140mg sod., 8g carb. (7g sugars, 0 fiber), 6g pro.

HAWAIIAN KIELBASA

HAWAIIAN KIELBASA

Savory sausage teams up with juicy, tangy pineapple for a winning combination you can prep in a flash. The sweet barbecue-style sauce is a tasty way to tie them together.
—Louise Kline, Fort Myers, FL

PREP: 15 MIN. • COOK: 2½ HOURS • MAKES: 12 SERVINGS

- 2 lbs. smoked kielbasa or Polish sausage, cut into 1-in. pieces
- 1 can (20 oz.) unsweetened pineapple chunks, undrained
- ½ cup ketchup
- 2 Tbsp. brown sugar
- 2 Tbsp. yellow mustard
- 1 Tbsp. cider vinegar
- ¾ cup lemon-lime soda
- 2 Tbsp. cornstarch
- 2 Tbsp. cold water

1. Place sausage in a 3- or 4-qt. slow cooker. Drain pineapple, reserving ¾ cup juice; set pineapple aside. In a small bowl, whisk the ketchup, brown sugar, mustard and vinegar. Stir in soda and reserved pineapple juice. Pour mixture over sausage; stir to coat. Cover and cook on low until heated through, 2-3 hours.

2. Stir in pineapple. In a small bowl, combine cornstarch and water until smooth. Stir into slow cooker. Cover and cook until sauce is thickened, 30 minutes longer. Serve with toothpicks if desired.

½ cup: 289 cal., 21g fat (7g sat. fat), 51mg chol., 975mg sod., 15g carb. (12g sugars, 0 fiber), 10g pro.

Jalapeno Peach Kielbasa: Substitute 1 can (20 oz.) unsweetened peaches for the pineapple. Add 2 thinly sliced fresh jalapenos. Proceed as directed.

SLOW COOKER

CRAB DIP

With just 10 minutes of prep time, this creamy crab dip couldn't be easier. The recipe comes from my hometown cookbook, and my co-workers rave about it at every company potluck.
—Julie Novotney, Rockwell, IA

PREP: 10 MIN. • COOK: 2 HOURS • MAKES: 2 CUPS

- 1 pkg. (8 oz.) cream cheese, softened
- ½ cup grated Parmesan cheese
- ½ cup mayonnaise
- 4 green onions, finely chopped
- ½ tsp. garlic powder
- 1 can (6 oz.) crabmeat, drained, flaked and cartilage removed
- ½ cup sliced almonds, toasted
- Assorted crackers

1. In a 1½-qt. slow cooker, combine the first 5 ingredients. Stir in crab. Cook, covered, on low until heated through, 2-3 hours.

2. Just before serving, sprinkle with almonds. Serve with crackers.

2 Tbsp.: 132 cal., 12g fat (4g sat. fat), 27mg chol., 185mg sod., 2g carb. (1g sugars, 0 fiber), 4g pro.

HONEY & ALE PULLED CHICKEN SLIDERS

Score big with your guests with a little bit of sweet heat! This recipe works well for game-day parties because the extra liquid in the slow cooker keeps the chicken tender and juicy all day long.
—Julie Peterson, Crofton, MD

PREP: 20 MIN. • COOK: 6 HOURS • MAKES: 12 SLIDERS

SLOW COOKER

- ¼ cup honey
- 2 Tbsp. cider vinegar
- 2 Tbsp. Sriracha chili sauce
- 1 Tbsp. chili powder
- 1 tsp. smoked paprika
- 1 tsp. garlic powder
- 1 tsp. onion powder
- ½ tsp. salt
- 2 lbs. boneless skinless chicken thighs (about 8 thighs)
- ¾ cup brown ale
- 3 Tbsp. cornstarch
- 3 Tbsp. water
- 12 slider buns
- Optional: Sweet pickles and additional Sriracha sauce

1. In a 3- or 4-qt. slow cooker, combine the first 8 ingredients. Add chicken and ale; toss to coat. Cook, covered, on low until chicken is tender, 6-8 hours. Remove meat; when chicken is cool enough to handle, shred with 2 forks.

2. Strain cooking juices; skim fat. Transfer juices to a small saucepan; bring to a boil. In a small bowl, mix cornstarch and water until smooth; stir into saucepan. Return to a boil, stirring constantly; cook and stir until thickened, about 5 minutes. Add chicken to the sauce; toss to coat. Serve on buns. Add pickles and additional Sriracha sauce if desired.

1 slider: 224 cal., 7g fat (2g sat. fat), 51mg chol., 357mg sod., 22g carb. (8g sugars, 1g fiber), 17g pro.

TEST KITCHEN TIP: While many cooks often use chicken breasts for shredded chicken sandwiches, chicken thighs are the better choice for this dish. The extra fat helps the meat stays moist and tender, even after a long time in the slow cooker.

HONEY & ALE PULLED CHICKEN SLIDERS

SIDES

BAKED POTATOES, PAGE 249

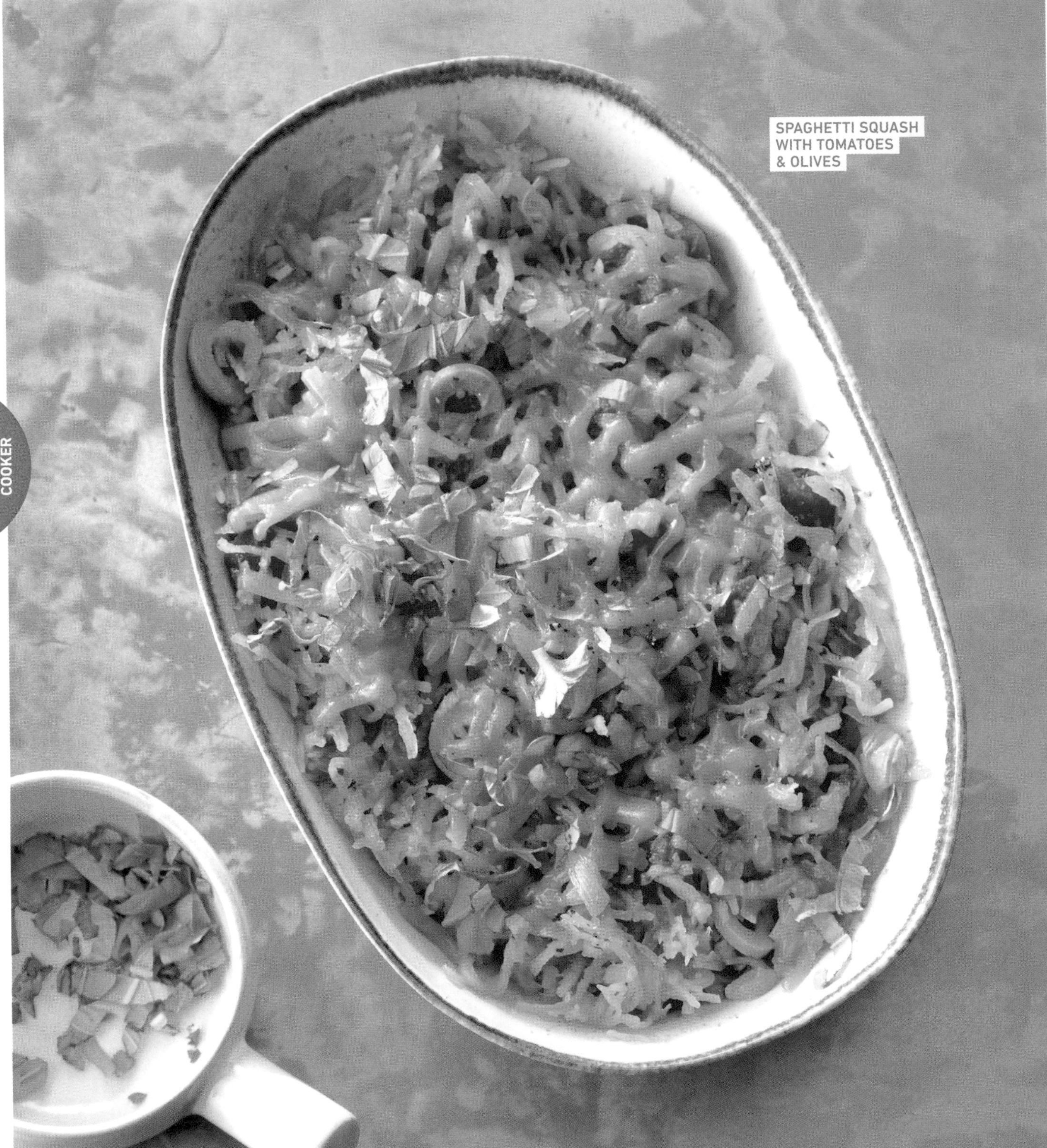

SPAGHETTI SQUASH WITH TOMATOES & OLIVES

SPAGHETTI SQUASH WITH TOMATOES & OLIVES

This spaghetti squash is outstanding as a side dish, but you can also top it with canned tuna to create a simple, healthy main dish. I use my own canned tomatoes for the best flavor.
—Carol Chase, Sioux City, IA

PREP: 15 MIN. • COOK: 5¼ HOURS • MAKES: 10 SERVINGS

- 1 medium spaghetti squash, halved, seeds removed
- ¼ cup sliced green olives with pimientos, drained
- 1 can (14 oz.) diced tomatoes
- 1 tsp. dried oregano
- ½ tsp. salt
- ½ tsp. pepper
- ½ cup shredded cheddar cheese
- ¼ cup chopped fresh basil

1. Place squash in 6- or 7-qt. slow cooker, overlapping as needed to fit. Cook, covered, on low until tender, 5-7 hours.

2. Remove squash from slow cooker; drain any cooking liquid. Using a fork, separate the squash into strands resembling spaghetti, discarding the skin. Return strands to slow cooker. Stir in the tomatoes, olives, oregano, salt and pepper; cook on low until heated through, about 15 minutes. Top with cheese and basil.

¾ cup: 92 cal., 3g fat (1g sat. fat), 6mg chol., 296mg sod., 15g carb. (1g sugars, 4g fiber), 3g pro. **Diabetic exchanges:** 1 starch, ½ fat.

TEST KITCHEN TIP: Adding the tomato mixture after cooking the spaghetti squash allows you to discard any condensed liquid from the slow cooker before combining all the ingredients.

SLOW COOKER

POLENTA

This Italian classic is so simple to make in the slow cooker. Now you can enjoy it any night of the week!

—Elisabeth Matelski, Boston, MA

PREP: 10 MIN. • COOK: 6 HOURS • MAKES: 12 SERVINGS

- 13 cups reduced-sodium chicken broth, divided
- 3 cups cornmeal
- 1 medium onion, finely chopped
- 3 garlic cloves, minced
- 2 bay leaves
- 2 tsp. salt
- 1 cup half-and-half cream
- 1 cup shredded Parmesan cheese
- ¼ cup butter, cubed
- 1 tsp. pepper
- Additional shredded Parmesan cheese

In a 6-qt. slow cooker, combine 12 cups broth, cornmeal, onion, garlic, bay leaves and salt. Cook, covered, on low, 6-8 hours, until liquid is absorbed and polenta is creamy. Remove bay leaves. Stir in cream, cheese, butter, pepper and remaining broth. If desired, serve with additional cheese.

1 cup: 255 cal., 8g fat (5g sat. fat), 25mg chol., 1168mg sod., 34g carb. (3g sugars, 2g fiber), 9g pro.

TEST KITCHEN TIP: Poletna is an Italian-style mush prepared from cornmeal and water and is often flavored with Parmesan or Gorgonzola cheese. It is cooked until thickened and smooth and served as a side dish much like rice or mashed potatoes. It's an ideal accompaniment to main dishes with sauce or gravy.

POLENTA

BAKED POTATOES

BAKED POTATOES

Here is the easiest way to make baked potatoes! Just cook the spuds in the slow cooker and then add your favorite toppings before serving. Save any extra potatoes to make baked potato soup the next day.
—Teresa Emrick, Tipp City, OH

PREP: 10 MIN. • COOK: 8 HOURS • MAKES: 6 POTATOES

- 6 medium russet potatoes
- 3 Tbsp. butter, softened
- 3 garlic cloves, minced
- 1 cup water
- Salt and pepper to taste
- Optional: Sour cream, butter, crumbled bacon, minced chives, guacamole, shredded cheddar cheese and minced fresh cilantro

1. Scrub potatoes; pierce each several times with a fork. In a small bowl, mix butter and garlic. Rub potatoes with butter mixture. Wrap each tightly with a piece of foil.

2. Pour water into a 6-qt. slow cooker; add potatoes. Cook, covered, on low 8-10 hours or until tender. Season and top as desired.

1 potato: 217 cal., 6g fat (4g sat. fat), 15mg chol., 59mg sod., 38g carb. (2g sugars, 5g fiber), 5g pro.

TEST KITCHEN TIP: Skip the high-calorie sour cream and try a dollop of fat-free Greek yogurt instead. (Don't forget to add a sprinkle of chives.)

EASY GREEN BEANS WITH MUSHROOMS

My family looks forward to this side dish every holiday.
I add sliced almonds for crunch and garlic for a little kick.
—Cheryl Wittman, Bergen, NY

PREP: 10 MIN. • COOK: 5 HOURS • MAKES: 10 SERVINGS

- 2 lbs. fresh green beans, trimmed
- 1 lb. sliced fresh mushrooms
- 1 large onion, finely chopped
- 2 Tbsp. butter, melted
- 2 Tbsp. olive oil
- 3 garlic cloves, minced
- ½ tsp. salt
- ¼ tsp. pepper
- ½ cup sliced almonds, toasted

In a 6-qt. slow cooker, combine all ingredients except the almonds. Cook, covered, on low 5-6 hours or until beans are tender. Remove with a slotted spoon. Top with almonds.

Note: To toast nuts, bake in a shallow pan in a 350° oven for 5-10 minutes or cook in a skillet over low heat until lightly browned, stirring occasionally.

1 serving: 116 cal., 8g fat (2g sat. fat), 6mg chol., 145mg sod., 11g carb. (4g sugars, 4g fiber), 4g pro.
Diabetic exchanges: 1½ fat, 1 vegetable.

SLOW COOKER

SMOKY HASH BROWN CASSEROLE

Making this delicious, savory casserole in the slow cooker saves space in the oven, and with just a few staple convenience items, it comes together easily.
—Susan Hein, Burlington, WI

PREP: 10 MIN. • COOK: 3½ HOURS • MAKES: 6 SERVINGS

- 1 tsp. butter
- 1 pkg. (28 oz.) frozen O'Brien potatoes, thawed
- 1 can (10¾ oz.) condensed cream of chicken soup, undiluted
- 4 oz. smoked cheddar cheese, shredded
- ½ tsp. pepper
- ¼ tsp. salt

Grease a 3-qt. slow cooker with butter. Combine potatoes, soup, cheese, pepper and salt. Transfer to prepared slow cooker. Cook, covered, on low until potatoes are tender, 3½-4½ hours.

¾ cup: 227 cal., 10g fat (5g sat. fat), 25mg chol., 626mg sod., 25g carb. (2g sugars, 4g fiber), 7g pro.

EASY GREEN BEANS WITH MUSHROOMS

LORA'S RED BEANS & RICE

LORA'S RED BEANS & RICE

My dear mother-in-law passed this simple recipe to me. With meats, beans and savory veggies that simmer all day, it's tasty, easy and economical, too!
—Carol Simms, Madison, MS

PREP: 15 MIN. + SOAKING • COOK: 8 HOURS • MAKES: 10 SERVINGS

- 1 pkg. (16 oz.) dried kidney beans (about 2½ cups)
- 2 cups cubed fully cooked ham (about 1 lb.)
- 1 pkg. (12 oz.) fully cooked andouille chicken sausage links or flavor of choice, sliced
- 1 medium green pepper, chopped
- 1 medium onion, chopped
- 2 celery ribs, chopped
- 1 Tbsp. hot pepper sauce
- 2 garlic cloves, minced
- 1½ tsp. salt
- Hot cooked rice

1. Place beans in a large bowl; add cool water to cover. Soak overnight.

2. Drain beans, discarding water; rinse with cool water. Place beans in a greased 6-qt. slow cooker. Stir in ham, sausage, vegetables, pepper sauce, garlic and salt. Add water to cover by 1 in.

3. Cook, covered, on low, until beans are tender, 8-9 hours. Serve with rice.

1 cup bean mixture: 249 cal., 5g fat (1g sat. fat), 43mg chol., 906mg sod., 31g carb. (2g sugars, 7g fiber), 23g pro.

TEST KITCHEN TIP: You can also use smoked turkey sausage in place of andouille chicken sausage.

CREAMY RANCHIFIED POTATOES

My daughter-in-law gave me this recipe and, over the years, I've adjusted it to our tastes. It's so nice to come home from work to a hot, tasty dish that's ready to serve. You can use any cheese you'd like and can also use leftover chicken or another meat in addition to, or in place of, the ham.
—Jane Whittaker, Pensacola, FL

PREP: 15 MIN. • COOK: 6 HOURS • MAKES: 8 SERVINGS

SLOW COOKER

- 2 lbs. small red potatoes, quartered
- 1 cup cubed fully cooked ham
- 1 can (10¾ oz.) condensed cream of potato soup, undiluted
- 1 carton (8 oz.) spreadable chive and onion cream cheese
- 3 Tbsp. minced chives
- 1 envelope ranch salad dressing mix
- 1 tsp. pepper
- 6 oz. pepper jack cheese, grated

In a 4-qt. slow cooker, combine the first 7 ingredients. Cook, covered, on low until potatoes are tender, 6-8 hours. Top with cheese; stir to combine.

¾ cup: 297 cal., 15g fat (8g sat. fat), 53mg chol., 933mg sod., 28g carb. (2g sugars, 3g fiber), 14g pro.

WHY YOU'LL LOVE IT...

"Delicious, creamy goodness! I didn't have cream cheese so I used sour cream and it turned out great. I also added fresh dill. The flavors mixed with our leftover ham made it a keeper!"

—HEIDIRVINE, TASTEOFHOME.COM

CREAMY
RANCHIFIED
POTATOES

MUSHROOM & RICE PILAF

MUSHROOM & RICE PILAF

This easy rice pilaf is a lifesaver on busy days. Just place the ingredients in the slow cooker and forget about it until it's time to serve!

—Kathleen Hedger, Godfrey, IL

PREP: 15 MIN. • COOK: 3 HOURS • MAKES: 10 SERVINGS

- ½ cup butter, cubed
- 2 cups uncooked long grain rice
- ½ lb. sliced fresh mushrooms
- 8 green onions, chopped
- 2 tsp. dried oregano
- 2 cans (10½ oz. each) condensed beef broth, undiluted
- 1½ cups water

In a large saucepan, heat butter over medium heat. Add the rice; cook and stir until lightly browned, 5-6 minutes. Transfer to a 3-qt. slow cooker. Add the mushrooms, green onions and oregano. Stir in the broth and water. Cook, covered, on low until rice is tender and liquid is absorbed, 3-4 hours.

¾ cup: 246 cal., 10g fat (6g sat. fat), 24mg chol., 470mg sod., 34g carb. (1g sugars, 1g fiber), 6g pro.

SLOW COOKER

GREEN CHILE CREAMED CORN

When hosting big dinners, I would often run out of burners on my stovetop. Then I realized my slow cooker could help by simmering up one of my side dishes. Corn and green chiles with pickled jalapenos is a favorite at many of our family gatherings.

—Pat Dazis, Charlotte, NC

PREP: 10 MIN. • COOK: 2½ HOURS • MAKES: 8 SERVINGS

- 6 cups fresh or frozen corn (about 30 oz.), thawed
- 1 pkg. (8 oz.) cream cheese, cubed
- 1 jar (4 oz.) diced pimientos, drained
- 1 can (4 oz.) chopped green chiles
- ½ cup vegetable broth
- ¼ cup butter, cubed
- ¼ cup pickled jalapeno slices, coarsely chopped
- 1 Tbsp. sugar
- ⅛ tsp. crushed red pepper flakes

In a 3- or 4-qt. slow cooker, combine all ingredients. Cook, covered, on low 2½-3 hours or until heated through. Stir just before serving.

¾ cup: 258 cal., 17g fat (10g sat. fat), 44mg chol., 296mg sod., 25g carb. (10g sugars, 3g fiber), 6g pro.

TEST KITCHEN TIP: Always fill your slow cooker to about ¾ capacity to prevent overcooking and overflow.

CHICKPEA TAGINE

While traveling through Morocco, my wife and I fell in love with the complex flavors of the many tagines we tried. Resist the urge to stir, as it will break down the veggies. To make it a main dish, add shredded cooked chicken in the last 10 minutes of cooking, or serve with grilled fish.

—Raymond Wyatt, West St. Paul, MN

PREP: 20 MIN. • COOK: 4 HOURS • MAKES: 12 SERVINGS

SLOW COOKER

- 1 small butternut squash (about 2 lbs.), peeled and cut into ½-in. cubes
- 2 medium zucchini, cut into ½-in. pieces
- 1 medium sweet red pepper, coarsely chopped
- 1 medium onion, coarsely chopped
- 1 can (15 oz.) chickpeas or garbanzo beans, rinsed and drained
- 12 dried apricots, halved
- 2 Tbsp. olive oil
- 2 garlic cloves, minced
- 2 tsp. paprika
- 1 tsp. ground ginger
- 1 tsp. ground cumin
- ½ tsp. salt
- ¼ tsp. pepper
- ¼ tsp. ground cinnamon
- 1 can (14.5 oz.) crushed tomatoes
- 2 to 3 tsp. harissa chili paste
- 2 tsp. honey
- ¼ cup chopped fresh mint leaves
- Plain Greek yogurt, optional
- Optional: Additional olive oil, honey and fresh mint

1. Place the first 6 ingredients in a 5- or 6-qt. slow cooker.

2. In a skillet, heat oil over medium heat. Add garlic, paprika, ginger, cumin, salt, pepper and cinnamon; cook and stir until fragrant, about 1 minute. Add tomatoes, harissa and honey; bring to a boil. Pour the tomato mixture over vegetables; stir to combine. Cook, covered, on low until vegetables are tender and sauce has thickened, 4-5 hours. Stir in mint.

3. If desired, top with yogurt, and additional mint, olive oil and honey to serve.

¾ cup: 127 cal., 3g fat (0 sat. fat), 0 chol., 224mg sod., 23g carb. (9g sugars, 6g fiber), 4g pro. **Diabetic exchanges:** 1½ starch, ½ fat.

TEST KITCHEN TIP: If you don't have harissa paste but still want some heat, add a little hot pepper sauce or crushed red pepper flakes.

CHICKPEA TAGINE

MEDITERRANEAN MASHED POTATOES

MEDITERRANEAN MASHED POTATOES

I love to use my slow cooker when family comes over for dinner. When I make my special turkey meat loaf on Sundays, I include this no-fuss side dish on the menu. It tastes amazing!

—Kristen Heigl, Staten Island, NY

PREP: 20 MIN. • COOK: 2 HOURS • MAKES: 10 SERVINGS

- 4 lbs. red potatoes, cubed
- 1 cup sour cream
- ½ cup butter, softened
- 3 garlic cloves, minced
- 2 Tbsp. snipped fresh dill
- ¾ tsp. salt
- ½ tsp. pepper
- 1 cup crumbled feta cheese

Place potatoes in a 6-qt. stockpot; add water to cover. Bring to a boil. Reduce heat; cook, uncovered, until tender, 10-15 minutes. Drain and coarsely mash. Combine next 6 ingredients in a greased 5-qt. slow cooker; stir in mashed potatoes and feta until well combined. Cook, covered, on low until heated through, 2-3 hours.

¾ cup: 287 cal., 15g fat (10g sat. fat), 46mg chol., 377mg sod., 30g carb. (3g sugars, 4g fiber), 6g pro.

TEST KITCHEN TIP: A bouquet of wispy, fragrant fronds, fresh dill weed has a fresh, sweet, grassy flavor.

SAUSAGE, KALE & SQUASH BREAD PUDDING

Who said bread pudding has to be for dessert? I serve this for brunch or dinner when I want something hearty and a little out of the ordinary.
—Lauren McAnelly, Des Moines, IA

PREP: 25 MIN. • COOK: 3 HOURS • MAKES: 12 SERVINGS

SLOW COOKER

- 1 lb. bulk spicy pork sausage
- 1½ cups chopped sweet onion (about 1 medium)
- 3 garlic cloves, minced
- ½ cup white wine
- 1 loaf sourdough bread (about 1 lb.), lightly toasted and cubed
- 4 cups chopped fresh kale
- 3 cups cubed peeled butternut squash
- 1 cup shredded Gruyere or Swiss cheese
- 1 cup chicken broth
- 4 large eggs
- ½ cup heavy whipping cream
- 1 Tbsp. minced fresh thyme
- 1 tsp. salt
- ½ tsp. coarsely ground pepper

1. In a large skillet, cook and crumble sausage over medium heat until it is no longer pink, 6-8 minutes. Remove sausage with a slotted spoon; drain on paper towels.

2. In the same skillet, cook and stir onion over medium-low heat until just softened, 2-3 minutes. Add garlic; cook 1 minute longer. Add wine, stirring to loosen browned bits from pan. Cook until liquid is almost evaporated, 2-4 minutes. Transfer to a large bowl. Add sausage, bread, kale, squash, cheese and broth; toss to combine.

3. In another bowl, whisk the eggs, cream, thyme, salt and pepper until blended. Pour over bread mixture; toss to coat. Transfer to a greased 6-qt. slow cooker. Cook, covered, on low 3-4 hours or until the squash is tender. Serve warm.

¾ cup: 330 cal., 17g fat (7g sat. fat), 104mg chol., 831mg sod., 28g carb. (4g sugars, 2g fiber), 14g pro.

SAUSAGE, KALE & SQUASH BREAD PUDDING

ENTREES

WEEKNIGHT GOULASH, PAGE 275

CURRY COCONUT CHICKEN

CURRY COCONUT CHICKEN

My husband and I love this yummy dish. It's a breeze to prepare in the slow cooker, and it tastes just like a meal you'd have at your favorite Indian or Thai restaurant.

—Andi Kauffman, Beavercreek, OR

PREP: 20 MIN. • COOK: 4 HOURS • MAKES: 2 SERVINGS

- 1 medium potato, peeled and cubed
- ¼ cup chopped onion
- 2 boneless skinless chicken breast halves (4 oz. each)
- ½ cup light coconut milk
- 2 tsp. curry powder
- 1 garlic clove, minced
- ½ tsp. reduced-sodium chicken bouillon granules
- ⅛ tsp. salt
- ⅛ tsp. pepper
- 1 cup hot cooked rice
- 1 green onion, thinly sliced
- Optional: Raisins, shredded coconut and chopped unsalted peanuts

1. Place potatoes and onion in a 1½- or 2-qt. slow cooker. In a large skillet coated with cooking spray, brown the chicken on both sides. Transfer to slow cooker.

2. In a small bowl, combine the coconut milk, curry, garlic, bouillon, salt and pepper; pour over chicken. Cover and cook on low for 4-5 hours, until meat is tender.

3. Serve chicken and sauce with rice; sprinkle with green onions. If desired, garnish with raisins, coconut and peanuts.

1 serving: 353 cal., 7g fat (4g sat. fat), 63mg chol., 266mg sod., 42g carb. (3g sugars, 3g fiber), 27g pro.

SLOW COOKER

BUFFALO PULLED CHICKEN

This slow-cooker recipe is one of my favorite go-to's for game days. Buffalo chicken breast is a nice alternative to traditional pulled pork.

—Kim Ciepluch, Kenosha, WI

PREP: 5 MIN. • COOK: 3 HOURS • MAKES: 6 SERVINGS

- ½ cup Buffalo wing sauce
- 2 Tbsp. ranch salad dressing mix
- 4 boneless skinless chicken breast halves (6 oz. each)
- Optional: Celery ribs or crusty sandwich buns, crumbled blue cheese, additional wing sauce and ranch salad dressing

1. In a 3-qt. slow cooker, mix wing sauce and dressing mix. Add chicken. Cook, covered, on low 3-4 hours or until meat is tender.

2. Shred chicken with 2 forks. If desired, serve on celery, top with blue cheese and additional wing sauce, and serve with ranch dressing.

½ cup chicken mixture: 147 cal., 3g fat (1g sat. fat), 63mg chol., 1288mg sod., 6g carb. (0 sugars, 0 fiber), 23g pro.

CHUNKY CHICKEN CACCIATORE

This recipe is so versatile. Look in your fridge for anything else you want to throw in, like red pepper, mushrooms, extra zucchini—you name it! Omit the chicken if you're a vegetarian.
—Stephanie Loaiza, Layton, UT

PREP: 10 MIN. • COOK: 4 HOURS • MAKES: 6 SERVINGS

- 6 boneless skinless chicken thighs (about 1½ lbs.)
- 2 medium zucchini, cut into 1-in. slices
- 1 medium green pepper, cut into 1-in. pieces
- 1 large sweet onion, coarsely chopped
- ½ tsp. dried oregano
- 1 jar (24 oz.) garden-style spaghetti sauce
- Hot cooked spaghetti
- Optional: Sliced ripe olives and shredded Parmesan cheese

1. Place chicken thighs and vegetables in a 3-qt. slow cooker; sprinkle with oregano. Pour sauce over top. Cook, covered, on low 4-5 hours or until the chicken is tender.

2. Remove chicken; break up slightly with 2 forks. Return to slow cooker. Serve with spaghetti. If desired, top with olives and cheese.

Freeze option: Place the first 6 ingredients in a freezer container and freeze. To use, place container in refrigerator 48 hours or until contents are completely thawed. Cook and serve as directed.

1 serving: 285 cal., 11g fat (2g sat. fat), 76mg chol., 507mg sod., 21g carb. (14g sugars, 3g fiber), 24g pro. **Diabetic exchanges:** 3 lean meat, 1½ starch.

WHY YOU'LL LOVE IT...

"This dish was so good! I have made it over and over again."

—DEBBIELARK, TASTEOFHOME.COM

SLOW COOKER

CHUNKY CHICKEN CACCIATORE

EASY POACHED SALMON

EASY POACHED SALMON

We had never tasted salmon until a friend told me about poaching it in a slow cooker. I tried her method and got moist, flaky results with little fuss. I added some soy sauce for extra flavor.
—Johnna Johnson, Scottsdale, AZ

PREP: 45 MIN. • COOK: 1 HOUR • MAKES: 8 SERVINGS

6 cups water
1 medium onion, chopped
2 celery ribs, chopped
4 sprigs fresh parsley
½ cup dry white wine
1 Tbsp. soy sauce
8 whole peppercorns
1 bay leaf
1 salmon fillet (3 lbs.)
Lemon slices and fresh dill

1. In a large saucepan, combine the first 8 ingredients. Bring to a boil; reduce heat. Simmer, covered, 30 minutes. Strain, discarding vegetables and spices.

2. Cut three 20x3-in. strips of heavy-duty foil; crisscross so they resemble spokes of a wheel. Place strips on bottom and up sides of a 7-qt. oval slow cooker. Pour poaching liquid into slow cooker. Carefully add salmon.

3. Cook, covered, on high 60-70 minutes or just until fish flakes easily with a fork (a thermometer inserted in fish should read at least 145°). Using foil strips as handles, remove salmon from cooking liquid. Serve warm or cold, with lemon and dill.

6 oz. cooked salmon: 266 cal., 16g fat (3g sat. fat), 85mg chol., 97mg sod., 0 carb. (0 sugars, 0 fiber), 29g pro.
Diabetic exchanges: 4 lean meat.

GREEK-STYLE STUFFED PEPPERS

The bountiful peppers found at the local farmers market in the early fall, combined with some standard Greek ingredients, create a dish that bursts with color and fresh flavor.

—Renee Murby, Johnston, RI

PREP: 30 MIN. • COOK: 4½ HOURS • MAKES: 8 SERVINGS

- 2 Tbsp. olive oil
- 1 small fennel bulb, chopped
- 1 small red onion, chopped
- 1 pkg. (10 oz.) frozen chopped spinach, thawed and squeezed dry
- 3 garlic cloves, minced
- 2 each medium sweet yellow, orange, red and green peppers
- 1 can (28 oz.) crushed tomatoes, divided
- 1 lb. ground lamb
- 1 cup cooked barley
- 1 cup crumbled feta cheese, plus more for serving
- ½ cup Greek olives, chopped
- 1½ tsp. dried oregano
- ½ tsp. salt
- ½ tsp. crushed red pepper flakes
- ½ tsp. pepper
- Chopped fresh parsley, optional

1. In a large skillet, heat oil over medium-high heat. Add the fennel and onion; cook and stir until tender, 6-8 minutes. Add spinach and garlic; cook 1 minute longer. Cool slightly.

2. Cut and reserve tops from peppers; remove and discard seeds. Pour 1 cup crushed tomatoes into bottom of a 6- or 7-qt. slow cooker. In a large bowl, combine lamb, barley, 1 cup feta cheese, olives and seasonings; add fennel mixture. Spoon mixture into peppers; place in slow cooker. Pour remaining crushed tomatoes over peppers; replace pepper tops. Cook, covered, on low 4½-5½ hours, until peppers are tender. Serve with additional feta and, if desired, chopped parsley.

1 stuffed pepper: 313 cal., 16g fat (6g sat. fat), 45mg chol., 684mg sod., 26g carb. (11g sugars, 8g fiber), 17g pro.
Diabetic exchanges: 2 starch, 2 medium-fat meat, 1 fat.

GREEK-STYLE STUFFED PEPPERS

WEEKNIGHT GOULASH

WEEKNIGHT GOULASH

With this recipe, you can put in a full day's work, run some errands and still get dinner on the table in hardly any time. Make it extra special by serving the meat sauce over spaetzle.

—Cyndy Gerken, Naples, FL

PREP: 25 MIN. • COOK: 8½ HOURS • MAKES: 2 SERVINGS

- 1 lb. beef stew meat
- 1 Tbsp. olive oil
- 1 cup beef broth
- 1 small onion, chopped
- ¼ cup ketchup
- 1 Tbsp. Worcestershire sauce
- 1½ tsp. brown sugar
- 1½ tsp. paprika
- ¼ tsp. ground mustard
- 1 Tbsp. all-purpose flour
- 2 Tbsp. water
- Hot cooked egg noodles or spaetzle

1. In a large skillet, brown beef in oil; drain. Transfer to a 1½-qt. slow cooker. Combine the broth, onion, ketchup, Worcestershire sauce, brown sugar, paprika and mustard. Pour over beef. Cover and cook on low 8-10 hours, until meat is tender.

2. In a small bowl, combine flour and water until smooth. Gradually stir into beef mixture. Cover and cook on high until thickened, about 30 minutes longer. Serve with noodles.

1 cup: 478 cal., 23g fat (7g sat. fat), 141mg chol., 1005mg sod., 20g carb. (14g sugars, 1g fiber), 45g pro.

SLOW COOKER

MESQUITE RIBS

When we're missing the grill during winter, these tangy ribs give us that same smoky barbecue taste we love. They're so simple, and fall-off-the-bone delicious, too!

—Sue Evans, Marquette, MI

PREP: 10 MIN. • COOK: 6½ HOURS • MAKES: 8 SERVINGS

- 1 cup water
- 2 Tbsp. cider vinegar
- 1 Tbsp. soy sauce
- 2 Tbsp. mesquite seasoning
- 4 lbs. pork baby back ribs, cut into serving-size portions
- ½ cup barbecue sauce

1. In a 6-qt. slow cooker, mix water, vinegar and soy sauce. Rub ribs with mesquite seasoning; place in slow cooker.

2. Cook, covered, on low 6-8 hours or until tender. Remove ribs to a platter. Brush with barbecue sauce; return to slow cooker. Cook, covered, on low until ribs are glazed, about 30 minutes.

1 serving: 314 cal., 21g fat (8g sat. fat), 81mg chol., 591mg sod., 7g carb. (6g sugars, 0 fiber), 23g pro.

GRAMPA'S GERMAN-STYLE POT ROAST

Grampa was of German heritage and loved the old-world recipes given to him by his mother. I made a few changes so I could prepare this dish in the slow cooker and give it a slightly updated flavor.
—Nancy Heishman, Las Vegas, NV

PREP: 20 MIN. • COOK: 6 HOURS + STANDING • MAKES: 8 SERVINGS

SLOW COOKER

- 4 thick-sliced bacon strips
- 1 lb. baby Yukon Gold potatoes
- 4 medium carrots, sliced
- 1 can (14 oz.) sauerkraut, rinsed and well drained
- ¾ cup chopped dill pickles
- 1 tsp. smoked paprika
- 1 tsp. ground allspice
- ½ tsp. kosher salt
- ½ tsp. pepper
- 1 boneless beef chuck roast (3 lbs.)
- 2 pkg. (14.4 oz. each) frozen pearl onions, thawed
- 4 garlic cloves, minced
- ½ cup stout beer or beef broth
- ⅓ cup Dusseldorf mustard
- ½ cup sour cream
- ½ cup minced fresh parsley

1. In a large skillet, cook the bacon over medium heat until crisp. Remove to paper towels to drain.

2. Meanwhile, place potatoes, carrots, sauerkraut and pickles in a 7-qt. slow cooker. Mix paprika, allspice, salt and pepper; rub over roast. Brown roast in drippings over medium heat. Transfer to slow cooker. Add onions and garlic to drippings; cook and stir 1 minute. Stir in beer and mustard; pour over meat. Crumble bacon; add to slow cooker.

3. Cook, covered, on low 6-8 hours or until meat and vegetables are tender. Remove roast; let stand 10 minutes before slicing. Strain cooking juices. Reserve vegetables and juices; skim fat. Return reserved vegetables and cooking juices to slow cooker. Stir in sour cream; heat through. Serve with roast; sprinkle with parsley.

1 serving: 552 cal., 31g fat (12g sat. fat), 127mg chol., 926mg sod., 28g carb. (9g sugars, 6g fiber), 39g pro.

GRAMPA'S GERMAN-STYLE POT ROAST

GINGER CHICKEN & QUINOA STEW

GINGER CHICKEN & QUINOA STEW

Ginger and soy sauce lend an Asian flair to this healhty one-pot chicken dinner. Serve it hot, cold or at room temperature.

—Doris Kwon, Newport Coast, CA

PREP: 25 MIN. • COOK: 3½ HOURS • MAKES: 8 SERVINGS

- 2 lbs. boneless skinless chicken thighs, cut into 1-in. pieces
- 1 cup quinoa, rinsed
- 1 medium onion, cut into 1-in. pieces
- 1 medium sweet yellow pepper, cut into 1-in. pieces
- 1 medium sweet red pepper, cut into 1-in. pieces
- 2 cups chicken broth
- ½ cup honey
- ⅓ cup reduced-sodium soy sauce
- ¼ cup mirin (sweet rice wine) or sherry
- 1 Tbsp. minced fresh gingerroot
- 2 garlic cloves, minced
- ¼ to 1 tsp. crushed red pepper flakes
- 1 can (8 oz.) unsweetened pineapple chunks, drained
- 3 green onions, thinly sliced
- 2 tsp. sesame seeds

1. Place the chicken in a 4- or 5-qt. slow cooker. Top with quinoa, onion and peppers. In a small bowl, whisk the broth, honey, soy sauce, mirin, ginger, garlic and red pepper flakes; pour into slow cooker.

2. Cook, covered, on low 3½-4 hours, until chicken is tender. Serve with pineapple, green onions and sesame seeds.

1 cup: 373 cal., 10g fat (3g sat. fat), 77mg chol., 696mg sod., 43g carb. (26g sugars, 3g fiber), 26g pro.

WHY YOU'LL LOVE IT...

"Absolutely delicious!"

—DWANNAD'ALLAGINO, TASTEOFHOME.COM

PULLED PORK SANDWICHES

You'll love the ease of this recipe—just throw everything in the slow cooker and get out of the kitchen. You hardly have to lift a finger for delicious results!
—Terri McKitrick, Delafield, WI

PREP: 15 MIN. • COOK: 7 HOURS • MAKES: 8 SERVINGS

- 1 can (8 oz.) tomato sauce
- 1 cup chopped onion
- 1 cup barbecue sauce
- 3 tsp. chili powder
- 1 tsp. ground cumin
- ½ tsp. ground cinnamon
- 1 boneless pork sirloin roast (2 lbs.)
- 8 seeded hamburger buns, split
- Optional: Sliced red onion, fresh cilantro leaves and dill pickle slices

1. In a 3-qt. slow cooker, combine the first 6 ingredients; add the pork. Spoon some of the sauce over pork. Cover and cook on low for 7 hours or until meat is tender.

2. Remove meat; shred with 2 forks. Return to slow cooker and heat through. Spoon ½ cup onto each bun. Serve with desired toppings.

1 serving: 322 cal., 10g fat (3g sat. fat), 68mg chol., 681mg sod., 29g carb. (9g sugars, 3g fiber), 28g pro. **Diabetic exchanges:** 3 lean meat, 2 starch.

SLOW COOKER

THAI PEANUT CHICKEN WITH NOODLES

I serve this Thai favorite with noodles mixed into the sauce, but it's also wonderful served over rice. Garnish with green onion or cilantro for a pop of color and fresh flavor.
—Catherine Cebula, Littleton, MA

PREP: 35 MIN. • COOK: 2½ HOURS • MAKES: 6 SERVINGS

- 1½ lbs. boneless skinless chicken breasts, cut into ¾ in. cubes
- 1 medium onion, chopped
- ¾ cup salsa
- ¼ cup creamy peanut butter
- 2 Tbsp. black bean sauce
- 1 Tbsp. reduced-sodium soy sauce
- 8 oz. uncooked linguine
- 1 Tbsp. canola oil
- ½ lb. sliced baby portobello mushrooms
- Thinly sliced green onions, optional

1. Place the chicken and onion in a 4-qt. slow cooker. Combine salsa, peanut butter, bean sauce and soy sauce; add to slow cooker. Cook, covered, on low 2½-3½ hours, until chicken is tender.

2. Meanwhile, prepare pasta according to the package directions. In a large skillet, heat oil over medium-high heat. Add mushrooms; cook and stir until tender, 6-8 minutes. Drain pasta; stir into slow cooker. Stir in mushrooms. If desired, sprinkle with green onions.

1⅓ cups: 378 cal., 11g fat (2g sat. fat), 63mg chol., 436mg sod., 37g carb. (5g sugars, 2g fiber), 32g pro. **Diabetic exchanges:** 4 lean meat, 2 starch, 2 fat, 1 vegetable.

PULLED PORK SANDWICHES

MEXICAN PORK
& HOMINY STEW

MEXICAN PORK & HOMINY STEW

This stew, also known as pozole, is a southwestern delicacy. I make it in the slow cooker so it can simmer on its own. The rich, brothy soup is full-flavored, much like a tamale in a bowl.
—Joan Hallford, North Richland Hills, TX

PREP: 30 MIN. • COOK: 6 HOURS • MAKES: 8 SERVINGS (2¾ QT.)

- 2 cups water
- 1 large poblano pepper, seeded and chopped
- 1 jalapeno pepper, seeded and chopped
- 1 can (14½ oz.) fire-roasted diced tomatoes, undrained
- 1 medium onion, chopped
- 4 garlic cloves, minced
- 2 tsp. ground cumin
- ½ tsp. dried oregano
- 2 lbs. boneless country-style pork ribs, cubed
- 1 can (29 oz.) hominy, rinsed and drained
- 2 cups reduced-sodium chicken broth
- 1 Tbsp. lime juice
- 1 tsp. kosher salt
- ¼ tsp. pepper
- Optional: Fried tortillas, cubed avocado, sliced radishes, lime wedges and minced cilantro

1. In a small saucepan, combine water, poblano and jalapeno. Bring to a boil. Reduce heat; simmer until tender, about 10 minutes. Remove from heat; cool slightly. Place mixture in a blender. Add tomatoes, onion, garlic, cumin and oregano; cover and process until smooth.

2. Transfer to a 5- or 6-qt. slow cooker. Stir in pork, hominy, broth, lime juice, kosher salt and pepper. Cook, covered, on low 6-8 hours or until pork is tender. If desired, serve with optional ingredients.

Freeze option: Freeze cooled stew in freezer containers. To use, partially thaw in refrigerator overnight. Heat through in a saucepan, stirring occasionally; add a little broth if necessary.

1⅓ cups: 257 cal., 10g fat (4g sat. fat), 65mg chol., 1005mg sod., 16g carb. (3g sugars, 4g fiber), 22g pro.

SLOW COOKER

POLISH KRAUT WITH APPLES

The combination of apples, sauerkraut and smoked sausage gives this hearty dinner an old-world flavor. It's delicious and easy to make.
—Caren Markee, Cary, IL

PREP: 10 MIN. • COOK: 3 HOURS • MAKES: 2 SERVINGS

- 1 cup sauerkraut, rinsed and well drained
- ½ lb. smoked Polish sausage or kielbasa, cut up
- 1 large tart apple, peeled and cut into eighths
- ¼ cup packed brown sugar
- ¼ tsp. caraway seeds, optional
- Dash pepper
- ⅓ cup apple juice

1. Place half the sauerkraut in an ungreased 1½-qt. slow cooker. Top with sausage, apples, brown sugar, caraway seeds if desired, and pepper. Top with remaining sauerkraut. Pour apple juice over all.

2. Cover and cook on low 3-4 hours or until apples are tender.

1 cup: 522 cal., 30g fat (10g sat. fat), 81mg chol., 1440mg sod., 49g carb. (41g sugars, 3g fiber), 15g pro.

SLOW COOKER

BARBECUE PULLED PORK SANDWICHES

My barbecue pork recipe is foolproof, and the results are wonderfully delicious. Just four ingredients and a slow cooker make a fabulous dish with little effort.
—Sarah Johnson, Chicago, IL

PREP: 15 MIN. • COOK: 7 HOURS • MAKES: 6 SERVINGS

- 1 Hormel lemon-garlic pork loin filet (about 1⅓ lbs.)
- 1 can (12 oz.) Dr Pepper
- 1 bottle (18 oz.) barbecue sauce
- 6 hamburger buns, split

1. Place pork in a 3-qt. slow cooker. Pour Dr Pepper over top. Cover and cook on low 7-9 hours or until meat is tender.

2. Remove the meat; cool slightly. Discard cooking juices. Shred meat with 2 forks and return to slow cooker. Stir in barbecue sauce; heat through. Serve on buns.

Freeze option: Place individual portions of cooled meat mixture and juice in freezer containers. To use, partially thaw in refrigerator overnight. Microwave, covered, on high in a microwave-safe dish until heated through, stirring occasionally; add a little water if necessary.

1 sandwich: 348 cal., 8g fat (2g sat. fat), 45mg chol., 1695mg sod., 43g carb. (22g sugars, 2g fiber), 25g pro.

POLISH KRAUT
WITH APPLES

SAUCY CHICKEN & TORTELLINI

SAUCY CHICKEN & TORTELLINI

This heartwarming dish is something I threw together years ago for my oldest daughter. When she's having a rough day, I turn on the slow cooker and prepare this special recipe.
—Mary Morgan, Dallas, TX

PREP: 10 MIN. • COOK: 6¼ HOURS • MAKES: 8 SERVINGS

- 1½ lbs. boneless skinless chicken breasts, cut into 1-in. cubes
- ½ lb. sliced fresh mushrooms
- 1 large onion, chopped
- 1 medium sweet red pepper, cut into ½-in. pieces
- 1 medium green pepper, cut into ½-in. pieces
- 1 can (2¼ oz.) sliced ripe olives, drained
- 1 jar (24 oz.) marinara sauce
- 1 jar (15 oz.) Alfredo sauce
- 2 pkg. (9 oz. each) refrigerated cheese tortellini
- Grated Parmesan cheese, optional
- Torn fresh basil, optional

1. In a 5-qt. slow cooker, combine first 7 ingredients. Cook, covered, on low 6-8 hours or until chicken is tender.

2. Stir in Alfredo sauce and tortellini. Cook, covered, 15-20 minutes or until tortellini is tender. If desired, top with Parmesan cheese and basil.

Freeze option: Freeze cooled, cooked mixture in freezer containers. To use, partially thaw in refrigerator overnight. Microwave, covered, on high, in a microwave-safe dish until heated through, stirring gently; add a little water if necessary.

1¼ cups: 437 cal., 15g fat (7g sat. fat), 91mg chol., 922mg sod., 44g carb. (8g sugars, 5g fiber), 31g pro.

ROSEMARY BEEF ROAST OVER CHEESY POLENTA

I love beef roast in the slow cooker, and it's fun to pair it with something a little different than standard potatoes. This is true comfort food!
—Elisabeth Larsen, Pleasant Grove, UT

PREP: 20 MIN. • COOK: 7 HOURS • MAKES: 8 SERVINGS

SLOW COOKER

- ¼ cup minced fresh rosemary
- 3 garlic cloves, minced
- 3 tsp. salt, divided
- 1 tsp. pepper
- 1 boneless beef chuck roast (3 lbs.)
- 1 Tbsp. canola oil
- 1 cup beef broth
- 2 cups water
- 2 cups 2% milk
- 1 cup cornmeal
- ½ cup shredded Parmesan cheese
- 3 Tbsp. butter, cubed
- Optional: Additional rosemary and Parmesan cheese

1. Mix rosemary, garlic, 2 tsp. salt and pepper; rub over meat. In a large skillet, heat oil over medium-high heat; brown meat. Transfer the meat a 5- or 6-qt. slow cooker. Add broth to skillet; cook 1 minute, stirring to loosen browned bits from pan. Pour over meat. Cook, covered, on low 7-9 hours or until meat is tender.

2. For polenta, in a large heavy saucepan, bring water, milk and remaining 1 tsp. salt to a boil. Reduce heat to a gentle boil; slowly whisk in cornmeal. Cook and stir with a wooden spoon until polenta is thickened and pulls away cleanly from sides of pan, 15-20 minutes. (Mixture will be very thick.) Remove from heat; stir in Parmesan cheese and butter. Serve with roast. If desired, serve with additional rosemary and Parmesan cheese.

1 serving: 471 cal., 25g fat (11g sat. fat), 130mg chol., 1216mg sod., 19g carb. (3g sugars, 1g fiber), 39g pro.

WHY YOU'LL LOVE IT...

"I have to say, this is the best roast beef I've made in a long time! The polenta was a perfect counterpoint to the beef. It's a new fave for both me and my husband."

—JENNIFER, TASTEOFHOME.COM

ROSEMARY BEEF
ROAST OVER
CHEESY POLENTA

CHICKEN
TINGA

CHICKEN TINGA

I first fell in love with this traditional Mexican dish at a taco stand inside a gas station. This is how I now make it at home. My version has a nice zing without being overly spicy.
—Ramona Parris, Canton, GA

PREP: 25 MIN. • COOK: 4 HOURS • MAKES: 8 SERVINGS

- 8 oz. fresh chorizo
- 1½ lbs. boneless, skinless chicken thighs
- 1 large onion, cut into wedges
- 1 can (14½ oz.) fire-roasted diced tomatoes
- ½ cup chicken broth
- 3 Tbsp. minced chipotle peppers in adobo sauce
- 3 garlic cloves, minced
- 2 tsp. ground cumin
- 1 tsp. dried oregano
- ½ tsp. salt
- 16 corn tortillas (6 in.)
- Optional: Shredded lettuce and pico de gallo

1. In a small skillet, fully cook chorizo over medium heat, breaking meat into crumbles, 6-8 minutes; drain. Transfer to a 3- or 4-qt. slow cooker. Add the next 9 ingredients; stir to combine. Cook, covered, on low 4-5 hours or until chicken is tender, .

2. Remove chicken; cool slightly. Shred with 2 forks. Remove and discard onions; strain cooking juices and skim fat. Return cooking juices and chicken to slow cooker; heat through. Serve chicken in corn tortillas. If desired, top with shredded lettuce and pico de gallo.

Freeze option: Freeze cooled chicken mixture in freezer containers. To use, partially thaw in refrigerator overnight. Heat through in a saucepan, stirring occasionally; add broth if necessary.

2 tacos: 363 cal., 16g fat (5g sat. fat), 82mg chol., 800mg sod., 27g carb. (3g sugars, 4g fiber), 25g pro.

TEST KITCHEN TIP: Chipotle peppers are dried and smoked jalapenos. They come canned in adobo sauce and can be found in the ethnic aisle of your grocery store.

SLOW COOKER

PIZZAIOLA MEAT LOAF

I add Italian Castelvetrano olives to the meat loaf mixture in this recipe. They're bright green, very mild and fruity, and are available in the deli section of the grocery store.

—Ann Sheehy, Lawrence, MA

PREP: 35 MIN. • COOK: 4 HOURS • MAKES: 8 SERVINGS

- 2 Tbsp. canola oil
- 1 large onion, chopped
- 1 cup chopped sweet red, yellow or green peppers
- 1½ cups sliced fresh mushrooms
- 2 garlic cloves, minced
- 2 large eggs, lightly beaten
- 1 cup seasoned bread crumbs
- 1 cup shredded Italian cheese blend
- 1 tsp. Italian seasoning
- ½ tsp. salt
- 1¼ lbs. ground turkey
- 1 lb. meat loaf mix (equal parts ground beef, pork and veal)
- Optional: Pizza sauce and shredded Parmesan cheese

1. Cut three 25x3-in. strips of heavy-duty foil; crisscross so they resemble spokes of a wheel. Place strips on bottom and up sides of a 5- or 6-qt. slow cooker. Coat strips with cooking spray.

2. In a large skillet, heat oil over medium-high heat. Add onion, peppers and mushrooms; cook and stir until tender, 4-6 minutes. Add garlic; cook 1 minute longer. Remove from the heat and cool slightly.

3. In a large bowl, combine eggs, bread crumbs, cheese, Italian seasoning, salt and reserved cooked vegetables. Add turkey and meat loaf mix; mix lightly but thoroughly. Shape mixture into a loaf; transfer to slow cooker. Cook, covered, on low 4-5 hours, until a thermometer reads at least 160°. Using foil strips as handles, remove meat loaf to a platter. If desired, serve with pizza sauce and Parmesan.

1 piece: 356 cal., 19g fat (6g sat. fat), 139mg chol., 551mg sod., 14g carb. (3g sugars, 1g fiber), 31g pro.

TEST KITCHEN TIP: Traditional pizzaiola is typically made with meat that's slow-simmered in tomato sauce until tender. The dish has a flavor that's similar to pizza. If you don't have meat loaf mix, this recipe can be made with all ground beef.

PIZZAIOLA MEAT LOAF

ENCHILADAS

ENCHILADAS

This fun stacked spin on traditional enchiladas will come in handy when you're craving southwestern food but don't have the time for extensive prep. It's sensational for busy weeknights.

—Mary Luebbert, Benton, KS

PREP: 30 MIN. • COOK: 5 HOURS • MAKES: 4 SERVINGS

- 1 lb. ground beef
- 1 cup chopped onion
- ½ cup chopped green pepper
- 1 can (16 oz.) pinto or kidney beans, rinsed and drained
- 1 can (15 oz.) black beans, rinsed and drained
- 1 can (10 oz.) diced tomatoes and green chiles, undrained
- ⅓ cup water
- 1 tsp. chili powder
- ½ tsp. ground cumin
- ½ tsp. salt
- ¼ tsp. pepper
- 1 cup shredded sharp cheddar cheese
- 1 cup shredded Monterey Jack cheese
- 6 flour tortillas (6 in.)
- Optional: Chopped tomatoes, minced fresh cilantro and sliced avocado

1. In a large skillet, cook the beef, onion and green pepper until meat is no longer pink; drain. Add the next 8 ingredients; bring to a boil. Reduce heat; cover and simmer for 10 minutes. Combine cheeses.

2. In a 5-qt. slow cooker, layer about ¾ cup beef mixture, 1 tortilla and about ⅓ cup cheese. Repeat layers. Cover and cook on low for 5-7 hours or until heated through. If desired, serve with optional toppings.

1 enchilada: 734 cal., 32g fat (16g sat. fat), 111mg chol., 1672mg sod., 62g carb. (6g sugars, 11g fiber), 49g pro.

WHY YOU'LL LOVE IT...

"One of the favorites in my house! Served with some sour cream and fresh guacamole on top. Loved it!"

—VIKTORIYAEHLERS, TASTEOFHOME.COM

MILK-CAN SUPPER

Here's a slow-cooked version of an old campfire classic. Pioneers and cowboys cooked this kind of meal in a milk can over an open fire, letting the flavors and textures blend together beautifully.

—Nick Iverson, Denver, CO

PREP: 20 MIN. • COOK: 6 HOURS • MAKES: 8 SERVINGS

- 1 Tbsp. canola oil
- 8 uncooked bratwurst links
- 2 lbs. small Yukon Gold potatoes, quartered
- 1 small head cabbage, coarsely chopped
- 2 medium onions, quartered
- 3 medium carrots, peeled and cut into 2-in. lengths
- 3 medium parsnips, peeled and cut into 2-in. lengths
- 6 fresh thyme sprigs
- 2 garlic cloves, crushed
- 2 bay leaves
- ½ tsp. salt
- ½ tsp. pepper
- 1 cup light beer
- 1 cup reduced-sodium chicken broth

1. Heat oil in large skillet over medium heat; add sausages and cook until browned, 3-4 minutes. Remove from heat; set aside.

2. Place potatoes in single layer on the bottom of a 6-qt. slow cooker. Top with cabbage, onions, carrots and parsnips. Add thyme, garlic, bay leaves, salt and pepper. Add sausages; pour beer and chicken broth over top. Cook, covered, 6-8 hours or until vegetables are tender. Remove bay leaves before serving.

1 serving: 457 cal., 27g fat (9g sat. fat), 63mg chol., 967mg sod., 37g carb. (6g sugars, 4g fiber), 15g pro.

TEST KITCHEN TIP: Parsnips are white root vegetables that have a creamy texture when cooked. Look for them in the produce section, near the carrots, in your grocery store.

MILK-CAN SUPPER

CUBANO SANDWICHES

CUBANO SANDWICHES

This recipe came about because I didn't have pepperoncinis for my usual Italian pork recipe, so I used pickles instead. It reminded me so much of a Cuban sandwich that I added the ham and Swiss cheese to complete the dish. Instead of adding cheese to the slow cooker, you can also build the sandwiches and top with sliced cheese. Place under the broiler to melt.

—Kristie Schley, Severna Park, MD

PREP: 15 MIN. • COOK: 6½ HOURS • MAKES: 8 SERVINGS

- 2 lbs. pork tenderloin
- 7 Tbsp. stone-ground mustard, divided
- 1 tsp. pepper, freshly ground
- 1 lb. fully cooked boneless ham steak, cut into ½-in. cubes
- 1 jar (16 oz.) whole baby dill pickles, undrained, sliced thick
- 2 cups shredded Swiss cheese
- 8 submarine buns, split

1. Rub pork with 3 Tbsp. mustard, season with pepper and place in a 5- or 6-qt. slow cooker. Add ham and pickles, including pickle juice. Cover and cook on low about 6 hours or until tender, turning halfway through.

2. Shred pork with 2 forks. Sprinkle cheese over meat mixture; cover and cook until cheese melts, about 30 minutes.

3. When ready to serve, slice rolls and toast lightly in a toaster oven or broiler. Spread remaining mustard evenly over both sides. Using a slotted spoon, top rolls with meat mixture. Serve immediately.

1 sandwich: 526 cal., 20g fat (8g sat. fat), 118mg chol., 1941mg sod., 36g carb. (4g sugars, 3g fiber), 48g pro.

WHY YOU'LL LOVE IT...

"Contest winner for me in this year's Crock-Pot throwdown! I followed the recipe exactly and it was a crowd-pleaser."

— DEVINSLEGESKI, TASTEOFHOME.COM

SLOW COOKER

SLOW COOKER

DESSERTS

BERRY COMPOTE,
PAGE 307

CHERRY UPSIDE-DOWN BREAD PUDDING

CHERRY UPSIDE-DOWN BREAD PUDDING

I've always loved bread pudding, and I enjoy fixing this for my family on a chilly day. Feel free to use another flavor of pie filling and omit the chocolate chips for a different variation.
—Ronna Farley, Rockville, MD

PREP: 20 MIN. + COOLING • COOK: 2¾ HOURS • MAKES: 12 SERVINGS

- 1 loaf (16 oz.) sliced white bread
- 1 can (21 oz.) cherry pie filling
- ½ cup butter, softened
- 1 cup sugar
- 5 large eggs, room temperature
- 2 cups 2% milk
- 1 tsp. ground cinnamon
- 1 tsp. vanilla extract
- ¾ cup semisweet chocolate chips
- Sweetened whipped cream, optional

1. Place bread slices on ungreased baking sheets. Broil each pan 3-4 in. from heat until golden brown, 1-2 minutes on each side; let cool. Cut slices into 1-in. pieces; set aside.

2. Spoon pie filling into a greased 5- or 6-qt. slow cooker. In a large bowl, cream butter and sugar until crumbly. Add 1 egg at a time, beating well after each addition. Beat in the milk, cinnamon and vanilla (mixture may appear curdled). Gently stir in chocolate chips and bread cubes; let stand until bread is softened, about 10 minutes. Transfer to slow cooker.

3. Cook, covered, on low until set and a knife inserted in the center comes out clean, 2¾-3¼ hours. Serve warm, with whipped cream if desired.

¾ cup: 393 cal., 15g fat (8g sat. fat), 101mg chol., 305mg sod., 58g carb. (27g sugars, 2g fiber), 8g pro.

WHY YOU'LL LOVE IT...

"Loved this recipe. The only change I made was that I omitted the chocolate chips. Even my niece who does not like bread pudding raved about this recipe. The recipe is a definite keeper."

—071246LM, TASTEOFHOME.COM

INDULGENT COCONUT RICE PUDDING

There's nothing better than a warm dessert during the cold months of winter. This rice pudding is a healthy option that doesn't sacrifice flavor or comfort. If you can't find turbinado or raw sugar, use brown sugar, adjusting to ¾ cup.

—Teri Rasey, Cadillac, MI

PREP: 10 MIN. • COOK: 4 HOURS + STANDING • MAKES: 12 SERVINGS

SLOW COOKER

- 1 cup uncooked long grain rice
- 5 cups coconut milk, divided
- 2 Tbsp. coconut oil
- 1 cup turbinado (washed raw) sugar
- 1 cup dried cranberries
- 2 tsp. vanilla extract
- 1 tsp. ground cinnamon
- Dash salt
- Optional: Toasted sweetened shredded coconut and additional coconut milk

Place rice in a 3- or 4-qt. slow cooker coated with cooking spray; pour in 4 cups coconut milk. Add coconut oil, distributing it evenly over top. Add next 5 ingredients. Cook, covered, on low until rice is tender, 4-5 hours, adding enough remaining coconut milk to reach desired consistency. Let stand, uncovered, 10 minutes. Serve warm, with toasted coconut and additional coconut milk if desired.

½ cup: 340 cal., 18g fat (17g sat. fat), 0 chol., 39mg sod., 43g carb. (28g sugars, 1g fiber), 3g pro.

TEST KITCHEN TIP: Try different flavors inspired by cuisine from other countries. For a taste of India, add a sprinkle of cardamom with golden raisins. For a taste of Thailand, cook it first, then stir in fresh mint and fruit such as mangoes and kiwis.

INDULGENT COCONUT
RICE PUDDING

BERRY
COMPOTE

BERRY COMPOTE

This is a decades-old recipe my grandma made when I was younger, and when I make it now, it reminds me of her. She always added extra blueberries to help thicken the sauce.
—Diane Higgins, Tampa, FL

PREP: 15 MIN. • COOK: 3 HOURS • MAKES: 4 CUPS

- ¼ cup sugar
- 2 Tbsp. cornstarch
- 1 cup water
- 1 can (15 oz.) pitted dark sweet cherries, undrained
- 1 pint fresh or frozen unsweetened blueberries
- 1 cup packed brown sugar
- ½ cup chopped walnuts
- ¼ cup all-purpose flour
- ¼ cup sliced almonds
- ¼ cup old-fashioned oats
- 1 tsp. ground cinnamon
- ¼ tsp. ground nutmeg
- Dash salt
- ½ cup cold butter
- Vanilla ice cream, optional

1. In a small bowl, mix sugar, cornstarch and water until smooth. Transfer to a greased 3-qt. slow cooker. Stir in cherries and blueberries. In a large bowl, combine brown sugar, walnuts, flour, almonds, oats, cinnamon, nutmeg and salt; cut in butter until crumbly. Sprinkle over fruit mixture.

2. Cook, covered, on high about 3 hours, until bubbly and thickened. If desired, serve warm with vanilla ice cream.

¼ cup: 256 cal., 12g fat (5g sat. fat), 20mg chol., 80mg sod., 37g carb. (30g sugars, 2g fiber), 2g pro.

NEW ENGLAND INDIAN PUDDING

My version of traditional New England Indian pudding is made in the slow cooker instead of the oven. Use real molasses—if it's too strong, cut the amount down to ⅓ cup.
—Susan Bickta, Kutztown, PA

PREP: 15 MIN. • COOK: 3½ HOURS • MAKES: 8 SERVINGS

- 1 pkg. (8½ oz.) cornbread/muffin mix
- 1 pkg. (3.4 oz.) instant butterscotch pudding mix
- 4 cups whole milk
- 3 large eggs, lightly beaten
- ½ cup molasses
- 1 tsp. ground cinnamon
- ¼ tsp. ground cloves
- ¼ tsp. ground ginger
- Optional: Vanilla ice cream or sweetened whipped cream

1. In a large bowl, whisk cornbread mix, pudding mix and milk until blended. Add eggs, molasses and spices; whisk until combined. Transfer to a greased 4- or 5-qt. slow cooker. Cover and cook on high for 1 hour.

2. Reduce heat to low. Stir pudding, making sure to scrape sides of slow cooker well. Cover and cook until very thick, 2½-3 hours longer, stirring once per hour. Serve warm with ice cream if desired.

⅔ cup: 330 cal., 9g fat (4g sat. fat), 83mg chol., 526mg sod., 51g carb. (36g sugars, 2g fiber), 8g pro.

TEST KITCHEN TIP: Most slow cooker recipes advise against lifting the lid and stirring during cooking. This recipe, however, requires periodic stirring to keep the edges of the pudding from getting too dark.

SLOW COOKER

NEW ENGLAND INDIAN PUDDING

TEQUILA POACHED PEARS

TEQUILA POACHED PEARS

It may seem like an unusual dessert to make with tequila, but it's deliciously refreshing with fresh pears and mint. Bring out this creative sweet when you want to impress dinner guests.

—Nancy Heishman, Las Vegas, NV

PREP: 20 MIN. • COOK: 4 HOURS • MAKES: 8 SERVINGS

- 2 cups water
- 1 can (11.3 oz.) pear nectar
- 1 cup tequila
- ½ cup sugar
- 2 Tbsp. lime juice
- 2 tsp. grated lime zest
- 1 cinnamon stick (3 in.)
- ¼ tsp. ground nutmeg
- 8 whole Anjou pears, peeled
- Sweetened whipped cream, optional
- Fresh mint leaves

1. In a large saucepan, combine the first 8 ingredients. Bring to a boil over medium-high heat; boil 2 minutes, stirring constantly.

2. Place pears in a 4- or 5-qt. slow cooker; add liquid. Cook, covered, on low until tender, 4-5 hours. Remove cinnamon stick and discard. Pour 3 cups cooking liquid in a small saucepan. Bring to a boil; cook, uncovered, until liquid is reduced to 1 cup, about 20 minutes.

3. Halve pears lengthwise and core them. Serve with sauce, whipped cream if desired, and mint leaves.

1 pear with 2 Tbsp. sauce: 155 cal., 0 fat (0 sat. fat), 0 chol., 3mg sod., 40g carb. (30g sugars, 6g fiber), 1g pro.

SLOW COOKER

STRAWBERRY RHUBARB SAUCE

This tart and tangy fruit sauce is excellent over pound cake or ice cream. I've served this topping many times and gotten rave reviews from friends and family.

—Judith Wasman, Harkers Island, NC

PREP: 10 MIN. • COOK: 6 HOURS • MAKES: 10 SERVINGS

- 6 cups chopped rhubarb (½-in. pieces)
- 1 cup sugar
- ½ tsp. grated orange zest
- ½ tsp. ground ginger
- 1 cinnamon stick (3 in.)
- ½ cup white grape juice
- 2 cups halved unsweetened strawberries
- Angel food cake, pound cake or vanilla ice cream

1. Place rhubarb in a 3-qt. slow cooker. Combine sugar, orange zest and ginger; sprinkle over rhubarb. Add cinnamon stick and grape juice. Cover and cook on low for 5-6 hours or until rhubarb is tender.

2. Stir in strawberries; cook 1 hour longer. Discard cinnamon stick. Serve with cake or ice cream.

½ cup: 111 cal., 0 fat (0 sat. fat), 0 chol., 5mg sod., 28g carb. (24g sugars, 2g fiber), 1g pro.

PEACHY SUMMER CHEESECAKE

Here's a cool and refreshing dessert that's fancy enough to take to any warm-weather gathering. You can make it ahead of time and freeze. Make sure you wrap it well so it's airtight, and add the peaches and whipped cream only after it thaws.

—Joan Engelhardt, Latrobe, PA

PREP: 25 MIN. • COOK: 2½ HOURS + CHILLING • MAKES: 6 SERVINGS

SLOW COOKER

- 1 pkg. (8 oz.) reduced-fat cream cheese
- 4 oz. fat-free cream cheese
- ½ cup sugar
- ½ cup reduced-fat sour cream
- 2 Tbsp. unsweetened apple juice
- 1 Tbsp. all-purpose flour
- ½ tsp. vanilla
- 3 large eggs, room temperature, lightly beaten
- 2 medium ripe peaches, peeled and thinly sliced

1. Pour 1 in. water into a 6-qt. slow cooker. Layer two 24-in. pieces of foil; roll up pieces lengthwise to make a 1-in.-thick roll. Shape foil into a ring; place in slow cooker to make a makeshift rack.

2. Grease a 6-in. springform pan; place on a double thickness of heavy-duty foil (about 12 in. square). Wrap securely around pan.

3. In a large bowl, beat cream cheeses and sugar until smooth. Beat in sour cream, apple juice, flour and vanilla. Add eggs; beat on low speed just until blended. Pour into prepared pan. Center pan on foil rack, not allowing sides to touch slow cooker. Cover slow cooker with a double layer of white paper towels; place lid securely over towels. Cook, covered, on low 2½ hours.

4. Turn off the slow cooker, but do not remove lid. Let stand 1 hour. Remove springform pan from slow cooker; remove foil from pan. Cool cheesecake on a wire rack 1 hour.

5. Loosen sides from pan with a knife. Refrigerate overnight, covering when cooled. To serve, remove rim from springform pan. Serve with peaches.

1 piece with 3 Tbsp. peaches: 268 cal., 12g fat (7g sat. fat), 129mg chol., 342mg sod., 27g carb. (25g sugars, 1g fiber), 12g pro.

PEACHY SUMMER CHEESECAKE

COCONUT MANGO
BREAD PUDDING
WITH RUM SAUCE

COCONUT MANGO BREAD PUDDING WITH RUM SAUCE

Topped with a brown sugar rum sauce, this Puerto Rican dessert is both exotic and familiar. It's even better with vanilla ice cream or whipped cream.

—Jennifer Jackson, Keller, TX

PREP: 30 MIN. • COOK: 3 HOURS. • MAKES: 6 SERVINGS

- 4 large eggs, room temperature, beaten
- 1 can (13.66 oz.) coconut milk
- ⅓ cup packed brown sugar
- 1 tsp. rum extract
- ½ tsp. vanilla extract
- ½ tsp. ground cinnamon
- 4 cups torn French bread
- ⅓ cup chopped dried mangoes
- ¼ cup unsweetened coconut flakes, toasted

SAUCE

- ¼ cup butter
- ½ cup packed brown sugar
- 2 Tbsp. water
- 1 large egg yolk, room temperature, beaten
- ½ tsp. rum extract
- Toasted unsweetened coconut flakes, optional

1. In a large bowl, whisk the first 6 ingredients until blended. Gently stir in bread, mango and coconut flakes. Transfer to a greased 3-qt. slow cooker. Cook, covered, on low until puffed and edges are dark golden, about 3 hours.

2. In a small heavy saucepan, heat butter and brown sugar over medium-low heat until blended. Whisk in water and yolk. Cook and stir until mixture is slightly thickened and a thermometer reads 175°, about 10 minutes. Do not allow to boil. Immediately transfer to a bowl; stir in rum extract. Serve warm bread pudding with rum sauce. If desired, top with additional coconut.

¾ cups with 2 Tbsp. sauce: 447 cal., 24g fat (18g sat. fat), 175mg chol., 285mg sod., 49g carb. (37g sugars, 1g fiber), 8g pro.

TEST KITCHEN TIP: Feel free to use whatever dried fruits you have on hand.

CRANBERRY STUFFED APPLES

Cinnamon, nutmeg and walnuts add a homey autumn flavor to these stuffed apples. What a lovely old-fashioned treat!

—Grace Sandvigen, Rochester, NY

PREP: 10 MIN. • COOK: 4 HOURS • MAKES: 5 SERVINGS

- 5 medium apples
- ⅓ cup fresh or frozen cranberries, thawed and chopped
- ¼ cup packed brown sugar
- 2 Tbsp. chopped walnuts
- ¼ tsp. ground cinnamon
- ⅛ tsp. ground nutmeg
- Optional toppings: Whipped cream or vanilla ice cream

1. Core apples, leaving bottoms intact. Peel top third of each apple; place in a 5-qt. slow cooker. Combine the cranberries, brown sugar, walnuts, cinnamon and nutmeg; spoon into apples.

2. Cover and cook on low for 4-5 hours or until apples are tender. Serve with whipped cream or ice cream if desired.

1 stuffed apple: 136 cal., 2g fat (0 sat. fat), 0 chol., 6mg sod., 31g carb. (25g sugars, 4g fiber), 1g pro. **Diabetic exchanges:** 1 starch, 1 fruit.

SLOW COOKER

CHOCOLATY PEANUT CLUSTERS

I turn to my slow cooker to prepare these convenient chocolate treats. Making candies couldn't be any easier!

—Pam Posey, Waterloo, SC

PREP: 25 MIN. • COOK: 2 HOURS + STANDING • MAKES: 6½ LBS.

- 1 jar (16 oz.) salted dry roasted peanuts
- 1 jar (16 oz.) unsalted dry roasted peanuts
- 1 pkg. (11½ oz.) milk chocolate chips
- 1 pkg. (10 oz.) peanut butter chips
- 3 pkg. (10 to 12 oz. each) white baking chips
- 2 pkg. (10 oz. each) 60% cacao bittersweet chocolate baking chips

1. In a 6-qt. slow cooker, combine salted and unsalted peanuts. Layer with remaining ingredients in order given (do not stir). Cover and cook on low for 2-2½ hours or until chips are melted, stirring halfway through cooking.

2. Stir to combine. Drop by tablespoonfuls onto waxed paper. Refrigerate until set. Store in an airtight container at room temperature.

1 piece: 205 cal., 14g fat (5g sat. fat), 3mg chol., 68mg sod., 18g carb. (15g sugars, 2g fiber), 5g pro.

CRANBERRY
STUFFED APPLES
SLOW
COOKER

INSTANT POT®

AIR FRYER

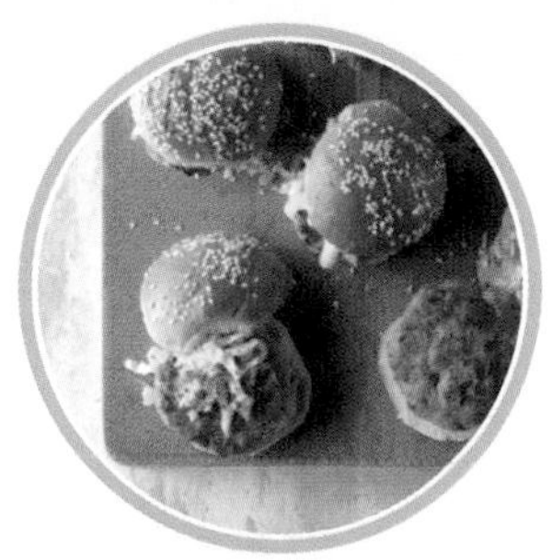

SLOW COOKER

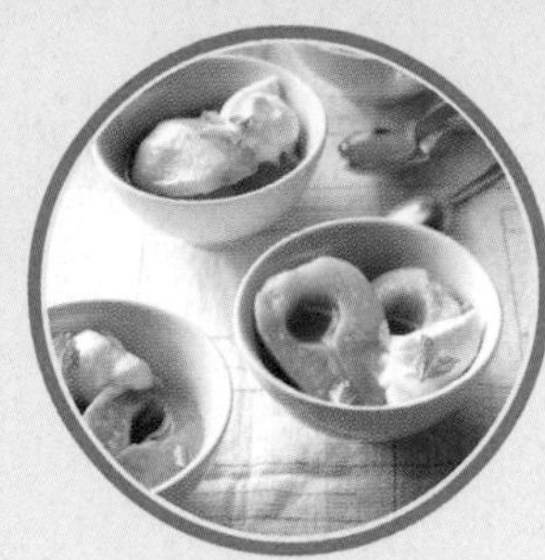